Wealth Logic

WISDOM FOR IMPROVING YOUR PERSONAL FINANCES

Moshe A. Milevsky, Ph.D.

Finance Professor
Schulich School of Business
York University

Revised and Expanded Columns
from the *National Post Business* magazine
January 1999–October 2002

Captus Press

Wealth Logic: Wisdom for improving your personal finances

National Library of Canada Cataloguing in Publication
Milevsky, Moshe Arye, 1967–
    Wealth logic : wisdom for improving your personal finances /
Moshe A. Milevsky.

Includes bibliographical references.
ISBN 1–55322–053–6

    1. Finance, Personal.   2. Financial security.   I. Title.
HG179.M5188 1999   332.024'01   C2002–905100–2

Captus Press Inc.
Mail: Units 14 & 15
        1600 Steeles Avenue West
        Concord, ON   L4K 4M2
        Canada
Telephone: (416) 736–5537
Fax: (416) 736–5793
Email: Info@captus.com
Internet: http://www.captus.com

Canada We acknowledge the financial
support of the Government of
Canada through the Book Publishing Industry
Development Program (BPIDP) for our publishing
activities.

0 9 8 7 6 5 4 3 2 1
Printed in Canada

Dedicated to the memory of my father.....

(Yerucham) Uziel Milevsky
1942–1992

NARAYAN, Ongkar
Feb 20, 1926 - Dec 15, 2020

Ongkar Narayan, a lifelong teacher and educator, passed away on December 15, 2020 at the age of 93.

He is survived by his loving wife, Manorama and children Narendra, Alita, Surendra, Keeran and seven grandchildren.

Ongkar was born in Essequibo, Guyana on February 20, 1926. He earned a B.A. from Susquehanna University in 1947, an M.A. in English from North East Missouri State in 1948, an M.A. in Secondary School Administration in 1956 and a Doctorate from Penn State University in 1972.

Ongkar was a devoted husband and father. He enjoyed playing cricket as a young man and made lifelong friendships during this time. He enjoyed traveling with his wife and visited many countries. His most defining characteristic was his willingness to help. Whether it be family, student or stranger, he provided support in whatever capacity he could and his kindness will live on. He will be deeply missed by all who knew him.

closely you may just hear his heavenly ba...
Mike created a connection with all who k...
and his zest for life! He has left his jo...
memory will live on in our hearts and in o...

A Virtual Memorial for Mike will be held o...
The link to this Service will be posted on...
Please email sherylm0808@gmail.com w...

SPILLETT, Ru...

It is with sadness that we share the ne...
2020 at the age of 95.

She will be lovingly remembered by ...
(Marion) and Joanne, grandchildren; ...
and great-grandchildren; Tricia, C...
predeceased by her husband Ken and ...

The family would like to express t...
assisted living staff at McConachie G...
care of Ruby.

Due to Covid 19 restrictions, a celebr...
date. In lieu of flowers, please consi...
Cancer Society or the Heart and Strok...

SE...
NOR...
WWW.s...

Table of Contents

Introduction: Go Yell at Him.   ix

1. Invest Like a Woman.   1
2. Does Picasso Belong in Your RRSP?   8
3. A Money-Back Guarantee on Your
   Mutual Fund?.   19
4. Dollar-Cost Averaging: Emotional
   Panacea or Logical Fallacy?.   26
5. How Much Should You Pay to
   Avoid MERs?.   33
6. Mortality Swaps: A Free Dinner?   39
7. Cloning with Derivatives.   45
8. Risk and Retirement   51
9. Investing with Other People's Money   57
10. What Is Financial Risk?   64
11. Are You an Active or Passive Investor? . .   71
12. Taxing Matters.   78
13. Insurance: When and Why   84
14. The Next Big Thing in
    Wealth Management   91
15. Managed Money's Catch 22:
    Juiced Returns and Stale Prices   95
16. Fund Fees and Frivolous Fights   100
17. So, How Much Do You Really Need
    at Retirement?   105
18. Are Options an Option?   110

19. Owning a Piece of the Local
    Gas Station 116
20. Stocks: In or Out (of the RRSP)? 122
21. Mortgages: Fixed or Floating? 130
22. Do Eggs Belong in Baskets? 140
23. Longevity Insurance: A Product
    Whose Time Has Come? 146
24. Hedge Funds: Do They Belong in
    Your Portfolio? 152
25. Trading Day and Night 157
26. Housing: Investment or Consumption? . . . 162
27. Car Leases and Hidden Options 168
28. You Are Wealthier Than You Think 173
29. Estates, Death and Taxes:
    To Insure or Not? 178
30. Credit Cards and Debit Dilemmas. 183
31. Mutual Funds: The Next Generation 189
32. The Rush To Leave:
    Is There a Money Drain? 192
33. Do You Want to Be Your Pension
    Fund Manager?. 198
34. Diversification: Is Anybody Listening? . . . 203
35. Ethical Investing: Can You Do Worse? . . . 208
36. Do Posted Rates Mean Anything? 212
37. Mutual Funds Rankings:
    Should Taxes Matter?. 216
38. Investing in Education 222
39. The Time and Value of Life Insurance. . . 227
40. Jewish High Holidays:
    A Time to Invest? 231

Bibliography 235

About the Author. 239

Futility of futility, all is futile. . . .

King Solomon, Ecclesiastes 1:1

Introduction: Go Yell at Him

December 25, 1992

My dear father, Dr. Uziel Milevsky — the former Chief Rabbi of Mexico City and world renowned Talmudic scholar — lay on a makeshift bed in the den of our family home in Toronto, dying of cancer at the untimely age of 50. My three younger brothers, our little sister and I, ranging in age from five to 25, had been standing vigil around his rapidly crumbling body, ever since doctors at Princess Margaret Hospital had admitted failure and sent him home a few days earlier. "Let his last days be in familiar surroundings," the helpful but defeated doctors had told us upon his release.

So we all knew that he was going to die. The only question for us — and for my father — was how quick and painful it would be for all involved. Most of the time during that last, terrible week at home, he was unconscious — or sleeping, as we told our precious sister, Debby. His rare moments of lucidity, which occurred every few hours or so, yielded cryptic and ambiguous remarks that we will interpret and cherish forever.

Tragically, a mere few months earlier, my charismatic and eloquent father collapsed immediately after one of his public sermons in front of hundreds of admiring disciples. A previously undetected brain tumour had invaded his nervous system and brought his oratorical career to a premature conclusion. Although surgeons later performed heroically in removing the tumour, it was not enough to save his life. The cancer had already metastasized — an ugly word that you should never have to hear or, worse, experience — and was slowly but steadily destroying his lungs and liver.

To the outside world, my father was a learned and distinguished authority. He had served as the Chief (Ashkenazi) Rabbi of Mexico during the early 1980s, and had lectured to thousands across five continents.

To the family, of course, he was all of that and much more. As the days came and went in that small room — and to help pass the time during that frightful deathwatch — my mother, my siblings and I held many discussions. Some were nostalgic and pleasant; others were frightening and tearful. As many people caught in such unfortunate circumstances can attest, young families form bonds that can last a lifetime.

During one of those sessions, in between the administration of endless morphine dosages, I remember the conversation veering towards money and finances. My parents never really shared much financial information with any of their children, let alone with me, their eldest son. Money was treated like sex. You knew it existed, you would experience it one day, but there was no need or urgency to discuss it today — and that was basically it. End of discussion.

So, despite my professional training in finance, economics and insurance, and although I would have been pleased to lend them advice at any time, I was completely ignorant of their monetary affairs. Now, with my father's condition quickly deteriorating, I was actually quite curious and more than a bit concerned. I was particularly worried about what would happen to my mother, Chaya. On what would she live? How would she continue to support my younger siblings? For most of her life she had stayed at home, raising the family and tending to community needs. We were never in penury, but nor were we rich. My father worked in the rabbinate all his life, which, despite the high profile, didn't really pay very well. I guess you were supposed to live on the "prestige and respect" of doing God's work. Indeed, at that time, I had three siblings still at home, all under the age of 15, which obviously left many mouths to feed.

Finally, I ventured a question. "What is the insurance situation? Do you know where all the important documents are? And who is the insurance company?" I wasn't going to ask about the face amount of the death policy — how much my father was actually insured for; it struck me as too personal and invasive.

It was then that my mother turned to me and said: "Oh, Ari," she always prefers my middle name, "your father didn't believe in life insurance. . . ."

My initial reaction was utter shock and disbelief. "No life insurance?" I replied, incredulous. "How could he not have life insurance?" Once again my mother explained it to me, as best she could: He just didn't believe in it. I was dumbfounded. "That's ridiculous," I protested in a bewildered haze. "Everybody has life insurance!"

"Go yell at him," retorted my perpetually acerbic brother, Jeremy. "He's lying right behind you."

This book. . . .

This book is dedicated to, and inspired by, my father — a man who taught me the value of logic, and the logic of value. This book is about the financial decisions we make in our daily life, and the personal risk management strategies behind them.

A few years ago, I was approached by the editor of the *National Post Business* magazine, who asked me if I was interested in writing a monthly column on the topics of personal finance, insurance and risk management. My broad mandate was to summarize interesting and relevant scholarly research — that might have been published in obscure academic journals — for a broader public audience. The only restriction he imposed was that my articles had to be exactly 720 words, since I had to leave room for a large and colourful piece of art, which would be related to the work in question.

At the time, I was flattered and honoured to be asked to step out of the ivory tower for a few hours each month, and I quickly agreed to the offer and to the relevant conditions. I have been happily writing a monthly column ever since.

Of course, little did I know how restrictive 720 words can be. At times, it felt as though the artwork was more important than the intellectual content, and I would groan when asked to trim words to make room for yet another colourful squiggle. In fact, I recall one instance when I was asked to change some numbers, since the existing ones didn't quite fit the artwork. . . .

But, with time — and with the help of my dear wife Edna, who is an accomplished artist herself — I learned to appreciate the importance of the visual effect and the need for more than just words.

I nevertheless always felt my ideas were being truncated, and I am happy to say that I finally have the opportunity to fill in the blanks.

This book contains 40 independent chapters that are all extensions of, or based on, brief articles I published in the *National Post Business* magazine during the last few years. While some chapters cover quite similar topics, they each contain a fresh idea. Indeed, without any numerical restrictions, I am now free to do a better job expressing views and opinions on the various topics that tickled my fancy over the last few years.

I would therefore like to take this opportunity to thank the editor of the *National Post Business* magazine, Tony Keller, as well as David Berman and Norah Murphy, for giving me the wonderful opportunity to share (720 words worth of) my writings with the Canadian public. Special thanks to Michael Posner, from *The Globe and Mail*, who helped launch my writing career and taught me much about bringing ideas down from the ivory tower.

While I'm on the topic of gratitude, I am indebted to my outstanding and supportive academic colleagues at the Schulich School of Business, the Faculty of Arts, and the School of Administrative Studies at York University. In particular I would like to acknowledge Kwok Ho, Elizabeth Maynes, Eliezer Prisman, David Promislow, Chris Robinson, Gordon Roberts, Tom Salisbury, Pauline Shum, and Bernie Wolf. They served as intellectual sounding boards over the years, while encouraging and tolerating my un-academic desire to communicate research ideas beyond the ivory tower. Their doors are always open, and I will continue to take advantage of that.

Also, I would like to thank Aron Gottesman and Diti Diena for helping me get through the process of converting a collection of short essays into a full-scale book. Last but not least, I would like to thank Mark Wolynetz, Randy Hoffman and the staff of Captus Press for making this book a reality.

. . . . And the remainder of the story

My father passed away a few days after our discussion about life insurance. As you can imagine, his death was very hard on our young family, leaving an emotional void that can never be entirely filled. But despite the absence of life insurance coverage, the financial implications were not as devastating as they might have been. You see, although my father did not buy any type of life insurance, he was very frugal, and not without financial acumen. He valued and saved every dollar he earned over his brief 25-year working life. And instead of spending a few hundred dollars per year on a life insurance policy, he had decided to invest those same dollars in a diversified portfolio of stocks, bonds and mutual funds.

In fact, as we later discovered, he owned mutual fund units in several top-drawer investment companies, including Dreyfus, Templeton and Fidelity. He also owned some gold and silver bullion, old stamps, ancient coins and some other bizarre investments that my mother has prohibited me from divulging in public.

Actually, we were happily surprised at the amount he had managed to amass and save on a rabbi's salary — with five children to feed. In the insurance lingo, my father had decided to self-insure. Instead of purchasing protection from a life insurance company, he opted to save and invest the premiums. He thus kept control of the money, and was able to exercise complete discretion as to how it was invested. Clearly, for this to work he had to actually save those insurance premiums, which requires a fair amount of self-control, which he certainly had.

Nevertheless, and with all due respect to my father's vast Talmudic wisdom, it was a lousy risk management strategy. Indeed, had he died earlier, he would have lost the self-insurance "bet". In fact, had he passed away 10 or 15 years earlier — during his thirties or forties, instead of at age 50 — he would have left the family destitute. This is despite his prudent saving and investing habits.

In my case, with three young daughters on the family payroll, I am not taking any self-insurance chances. In fact, one of the first things I did when I found out my wife Edna was pregnant with my eldest daughter was to rush out and get some life insurance. Yes, it might seem like an odd thing to do upon getting such wonderful news. But I realized that the present value of my liabilities had just increased by a couple of hundred thousand dollars, and I certainly didn't want to repeat my dad's mistake.

In fact, I'm sure that each and every one of you has a *personal* personal-finance story that epitomizes your own attitude towards risk and return. Perhaps it was a parent or uncle who lost it all on a bad real estate deal. Or, maybe it was a brother who was one digit away from winning the lottery, or maybe even a spouse who should have sold the stock, a day later, or a day earlier. These stories become urban family legends and form the psychological basis of an entire family's approach to money.

It is my sincere hope that this book will go some way towards helping you find the right balance between consumption and investment in your own life. My objective is to simply get you to think — on a deeper level — about many of the financial transactions you conduct on a daily basis.

I hope you enjoy.

Invest Like a Woman

1

I recall a phone conversation a few years ago with my mother-in-law. She had called from Ottawa to urge me to pull money out of those "silly" index funds and purchase some shares in JDS Uniphase, "for the children's sake." Although a teacher by training, her investment portfolio had apparently been doing quite well that year.

During the conversation I was reminded of the apocryphal story of J.P. Morgan (or was it Senator Kennedy?) and the shoeshine boy, back in the summer of 1929. Apparently, once Morgan started getting stock tips on the curb, he decided the market had peaked and it was time to sell. As we all know, he had perfect timing, and by chance my mother-in-law's conversation coincided with the peak of the technology boom as well.

But in all honesty, can my mother-in-law be better than me, when it comes to picking stocks?

Well, some academics have recently suggested that I start paying more attention to her choices. These studies conclude that, when it comes to investing, females do better than males.

One particularly interesting study looked at stock brokerage data and account activity from over 35,000 households in the western United States, during the period from 1991 to 1997.

The authors split the data according to whether the primary account holder was single or married, as well as whether they were male or female. Once these four categories were identified, the authors looked at the average gross and net return earned by the account over the period in question.

The term "gross return" refers to the increase in value before trading related expenses, such as transaction costs, are deducted. "Net return" is the increase in value after deducting trading related expenses. While the gross return associated with a portfolio may be high, the net return may be significantly lower, depending on the frequency with which trades are made. The more frequently the investor trades, the higher the trading related expenses, and the lower the net returns. A passive investor, on the other hand, who does not turnover the portfolio frequently, will have low trading related expenses, and will therefore have net returns similar to gross returns.

The results of their study are quite revealing. They suggest that although males and females earn similar gross investment returns, males tend to trade more frequently, take more risks, and invest in smaller capitalization stocks than females. But while gross returns are similar, females earn superior net returns, after deducting trading related expenses.

In other words, males tend to invest in sexier, more exciting stocks: smaller companies with uncertain futures. These stocks may perform fabulously well, but have a greater likelihood of failing. Further, males tend to change their mind about stocks more frequently, changing the nature of their portfolios through buying and selling individual stocks. These transactions are costly, and diminish net returns.

Women tend to invest in stability: larger firms with enough of a track record that the likelihood of failure is lower. And they tend to stick with their choices for longer periods of time, avoiding turnover.

Through reduced turnover, females decrease turnover costs, thereby increasing net returns.

Hence, we are more likely to find men investing in the stereotypical high-tech start-up for short periods of time. These are firms with few assets, no proven track record of profits or, even, revenues — but promises of gold at the end of the rainbow. Women are more likely to avoid such an investment, and will instead choose stable firms with a proven track record of profits — and stick with their decision.

The authors of the study argue that on a benchmark-adjusted basis, females are better investors than males. In fact, once marital status is taken into account, single males are the worst investors, while single females are the best. Overall, whether married or single, females earned approximately 1.1% per annum more than their male counterparts.

What exactly do I mean by "benchmark-adjusted basis"?

To explain, keep in mind that investing is, ultimately, a series of choices, and performance is measured by how well these choices are made. Some choices are obvious: For example, the choice of investing in equities instead of debt securities, or the choice to invest in international versus domestic securities.

Other choices are less obvious: For example, the decision to engage in "stock picking". There is, after all, an alternative: One can always take a "passive" approach, and simply invest in an index, such as the TSE 300 or the S&P 500, or any other passive index. Choosing to engage in stock picking — an "active" approach — is a choice the investor must make.

Now, since the investor has a choice whether to engage in stock picking or not, portfolio performance must be measured relative to benchmark performance.

For example, if I told you I carefully picked stocks for my portfolio on a weekly basis, and earned

23% on my portfolio last year, you would likely be quite impressed. Indeed, you might assume I am some sort of investment guru!

But what if the TSE 300 earned 35% over the same period? Suddenly, my 23% return doesn't look so fabulous. Indeed, 23% is 12% lower than the benchmark. In other words, by simply taking a passive approach (i.e., doing nothing except watch my money grow), I could have earned 12% more than my tedious, active approach.

My point is, you can't judge performance in a vacuum. Instead, portfolio performance must be judged relative to the choice you didn't make — the choice to invest in a benchmark portfolio. To do so, we calculate benchmark-adjusted returns.

Benchmark-adjusted returns means that gross returns are reduced by the returns of the passive portfolio the investor could have chosen to hold at the beginning of the year. This is a way of measuring the benefits from trading, as opposed to simply buying and holding.

In the earlier example, the benchmark-adjusted return is minus 12%, even though actual return is 23%.

Let's consider another example. If the benchmark portfolio you could have chosen to hold on January 1 lost 10% during the ensuing year, but you — after buying and selling over the year — lost 8%, then your benchmark-adjusted return is 2%. We see that on a benchmark-adjusted basis, negative returns may actually be good news!

Table 1 provides a summary of the excess return breakdown depending on the gender and marital status of the primary account holder.

The interesting question, of course, is, "why the difference?" Is there any reason why females should be better benchmark-adjusted investors than males, or is it simply a statistical anomaly?

TABLE 1
Females' Excess Investment Returns over Males

All Females	1.1% per annum
Married Females	0.9% per annum
Single Females	1.7% per annum

Source: B.M. Barber and T. Odean, "Boys will be Boys: Gender, Overconfidence, and Common Stock Investment," *Quarterly Journal of Economics* 116, 1 (February 2001): 261–92.

Well, one explanation offered by the behavioural finance psychologists is as follows. It seems that males and females choose their investments the way they choose their mates! Males look for excitement, females for stability.

Hence, while females tend to be more conservative and risk averse in their investment choices, males exhibit more overconfidence than females. Indeed, males tend to overestimate the precision and validity of their knowledge because they take too much credit for their previous successes. The clinical term for this behaviour is "self-serving attribution bias".

It's a dangerous scenario indeed: Males believe that past investment success is due to their "stock picking abilities", when in reality their success is pure dumb luck.

But is it really luck? Surely some males (and some females, for that matter) must have superior stock picking abilities? After all, we have all heard of people making it rich on the stock market!

Finance theory argues that it is, indeed, luck, and nothing more. Ultimately, investing in a stock is similar to any other gamble: You have your expected payoff, and you have your actual payoff. The expected payoff is the return you expect to receive. The actual payoff is contingent on the results of the variable upon which you base the gamble. Simply earning an actual payoff larger than the expectation does not indicate superior gambling ability. It simply indicates that you got lucky — and your luck can turn against you the next time you gamble.

But some males fail to recognize that past success is due to luck, and believe that past successes indicate superior abilities. This, in turn, causes males to gamble again — to trade excessively, which, to their detriment, reduces their benchmark-adjusted returns.

This story is confirmed by the above-mentioned study of 35,000 accounts, where females turned over their stock portfolio 53% annually, while males had a 77% turnover rate.

But why does marital status matter? As we noted earlier, single males are the worst investors, while single females are the best.

We may be able to explain tongue-in-cheek the significance of marital status through arguing that there is a contagion effect when males and females marry: Males may take on characteristics of their female partners, and start investing more wisely. Females, on the other hand, may get infected with the same hubris their male partners display, and start making irrational investment decisions.

In sum, although females and males tend to earn the same gross returns over time, females do so with more conservative stocks and with lower turnover. Therefore, on a benchmark-adjusted basis, the females come out ahead, by about 1% to 2% annually, as the above table reveals. An additional benefit of having lower turnover rates is that females can defer taxes in non-registered accounts and thereby increase their relative after-tax performance. As the authors noted, trading can be hazardous to your wealth, but more so for males than females.

As you can imagine, this type of result has important implications for money management world wide, and further research on "gender economics" is going on as we speak.

Do remember, though, to take these results in perspective. We are not talking about huge effects here, nor do we have a good understanding of precisely why this is happening and whether it will continue (or persist) in the future. So, please don't rush to dump your (single) male mutual fund portfolio manager in favour of a (single) female one. Rather, what I take away is that excessive trading seems to be a male trait — and can be hazardous to your wealth.

Does Picasso Belong in Your RRSP?

My wife Edna doesn't care much for the annual RRSP season. Every year she groans about what she perceives to be a waste of money, and for which I only have a formal piece of paper to show. You see, she is an artist by trade, and would much rather see the money go towards a nice painting or modern print, as opposed to being tucked away in a savings account or mutual fund. Unfortunately, the Canada Customs and Revenue Agency isn't quite ready to permit works of art in our retirement savings plans. (Although they still allow you to donate them to charity, at ridiculously inflated prices.) But this does bring to mind an interesting question. Is art a good investment?

Indeed, it is difficult to ignore the stories of well-known paintings selling for tens of millions of dollars. In fact, up to a few years ago, the British Rail Pension Fund (UK) maintained a large portfolio of art, solely as an investment, in the hopes of beating inflation. What's more, during the 1980s, Japanese investors were notorious for buying million-dollar artworks and just storing them in bank vaults.

So, is it time to set up a Canadian art mutual fund? Should you convert your G7 growth fund to a Group of Seven income fund? Is it time for the investment management industry to start hiring Ph.D.'s in art, to evaluate and manage art portfolios? There is a precedent: The industry has been hiring Ph.D.'s in biotechnology for years now to evaluate opportunities in the biotech industry.

Unfortunately for the art aficionados in the investment management industry, it appears the answer is a resounding "no".

A colleague of mine at the Schulich School of Business, Pauline Shum, took a rigorous look at the art market a few years ago, and her conclusions were revealing. She, together with a co-researcher at the University of Toronto, carefully constructed a 20-year semi-annual price index of repeat-auction Picasso prints. They chose Picasso because of the large volume of his outstanding work, and because Picasso prices are representative of the modern print market as a whole.

In contrast with the stock market, the art market isn't particularly efficient or rational, as you might imagine. General art prices peaked in 1990, and subsequently fell by almost 40%. Furthermore, at times, virtually identical prints can sell for different prices depending on where they are auctioned. Apparently, the same print might sell for 15% more at Sotheby's than at Christie's, and 10% more in North America than in Europe.

In the stock market, this type of anomaly would have long ago been arbitraged away. Arbitrage is an investment strategy where securities or assets are purchased for a lower price from one source, and immediately sold for a higher price to another. Because the securities or assets are immediately purchased and sold, pure arbitrage is risk-free. For example, if a stock is cross listed on two markets, say the NYSE and TSE, and the currency-adjusted prices differ, then an arbitrageur can take advantage of the discrepancy through purchasing the asset at the lower price on one market and selling it immediately on the other market. This should lead to an immediate risk-

TABLE 2		
In U.S. Dollars	*After-Inflation Return*	*Volatility*
Picasso Prints	1.48%	21.86%
U.S. Treasury Bills	2.29%	2.45%
U.S. Stocks	9.13%	16.84%

Correlation: Picasso & U.S. Stocks: +0.185
Picasso & U.S. T-Bills: −0.02

Source: J.E. Pesando and P.M. Shum, "The Returns to Picasso's Prints," *Journal of Cultural Economics* (1999), vol. 23.

free profit, assuming that transaction costs are not prohibitive.

Yet, despite this market's peculiarities, the researchers' main conclusion was definitive. After examining 20 years of Picasso prints, they concluded that your savings dollars are best placed elsewhere. In fact, you might say that a GIC would outperform Picasso.

To directly compare the investment benefits of art with other asset classes, Table 2 displays the real (after-inflation) rates of return from a portfolio of Picasso prints. For illustrative purposes, they are contrasted with the long-term investment returns from U.S. stocks and treasury bills.

Modern finance theory argues that we should expect a risk–return tradeoff when investing: The higher risk associated with one's diversified portfolio, the greater the expected return the portfolio should provide. This theory holds for U.S. T-Bills versus U.S. stocks: U.S. T-Bills have much lower volatility than U.S. stocks. Correspondingly, U.S. T-Bill returns have much lower returns than U.S. stocks.

Because of the risk–return tradeoff, I can easily understand arguments in favour of investing in either U.S. T-Bills or U.S. stocks. A rational argument can be made in favour of investing in U.S. T-Bills: An investor is willing to "pay" for his or her aversion to risk, in terms of lower expected returns. A rational argument can also be made in favour of investing in U.S. stocks: An investor is willing to accept risk in order to receive compensation in terms of greater expected returns.

However, it is quite difficult to argue in favour of an investment that combines high risk and low expected return. From an investment perspective, why accept such high risk, when lower-risk investments earn the same return? And if you must accept risk, why not choose a similarly risky investment that earns much higher returns?

This is why investing in the Picasso prints is not a good investment decision. It is quite evident that despite the very high volatility, the after-inflation return from Picasso prints is lower than the return from U.S. treasury bills. In the lingo of modern finance theory, the return does not compensate for the risk. In fact, on a year-by-year basis, the returns from the stock market are higher, yet less volatile, than the returns from the art markets.

The price index in this study is limited, as it considers Picasso prints exclusively. However, these results are fully consistent with previous research on the non-print art market. Academic opinion seems to be unanimous; the investment benefits associated with these assets, in terms of returns, are not worth the huge volatility. In fact, another major study found that the return from masterpiece paintings over a 400-year period was less than 0.50% after inflation.

Do these studies mean that buying (as opposed to investing) in the art market is never a good decision? Indeed, some investments in the art market pay off handsomely. Not long ago, I read a newspaper article about a painting that was auctioned off at Sotheby's in London for almost two million British Pounds — a work by 20th century artist L.S. Lowry. It is stories such as these that gallery owners love to tell and that naturally inspire collectors, for no doubt the Lowry painting was put up for auction by someone who had paid a fraction of that price to acquire it and made a healthy capital gain. But as the article pointed out, the Lowry story is the exception that proves the rule. For every work that raises millions in the hot-house environment of a public auction, there are a hundred or, far more likely, thousands that essentially disappear, having less or no greater value 50 years after they were painted than when they were first created or purchased.

This, then, is the first and overarching rule of investing in art: The odds of achieving significant capital appreciation are significantly against you.

Of course, when you think about it, this rule makes perfect sense. Every day, in every part of the world, tens of thousands of artists create new works in various mediums — oils, watercolours, sculpture and ceramics. In fact, my beautiful and talented artist wife Edna spends most her time painting. Our walls are covered with her lovely work. Most of these artists are extremely talented; no one questions that. But how many of them ever acquire even a modicum of recognition or renown? Very few. Statistically, the likelihood of any given artist gaining fame and high prices is remote. Most languish in galleries or in the artists' own workshops for years, gathering dust.

From an investment standpoint, the best analogy I can think of is professional hockey. Across Canada, the United States and Europe, literally tens of thousands of young boys start their journey towards the pro ranks as early as four and five years old. By their early teens, other interests have lured many of them away, raw talent has separated out many more, and some have been injured. But thousands remain, still fixated on their cherished goal of playing in the National Hockey League. How many actually make it? A small fraction of the original number. There are 30 teams in the NHL, each with (let's be generous) 25 players. That's approximately 750 players.

Buying the work of a young artist is like trying to guess who will be a pro hockey player when he is still 13 or 14 years old. It's not impossible, but the odds are stacked against them. The vast majority simply won't get there.

It is this rule, therefore, that you must keep firmly in mind if and when, like many eager investors, you adopt what I call the Buy Contemporary strategy. The appeal of such a strategy is obvious. If you buy modern young artists, you will almost certainly pay less for their work than you would for that of older, more established painters. In effect, you think, their careers — and the value of their canvases — have nowhere to go but up.

Let's say that you find an artist who you think is gifted. He or she has recently graduated from art school. The paintings sell for between $300 and $1,000 — for your budget, let's further assume, very affordable. Perhaps the artist has won small prizes, evidence (you conclude) that objective experts think he or she has talent. Perhaps he or she has been written up positively in the local press. What, then, is your downside risk? For $1,000, you're willing to take the bet and gamble that this artist will one day pay you a nice dividend on your investment.

To which I say, go ahead; don't let me stand in your way, especially if you think the work has aesthetic value. But understand that the chances of even doubling your money — turning your $1,000 investment into $2,000, let alone something more dramatic — are negligible. The cold hard truth is this:

It's unlikely the young artist will ever gain major-league fame. Most young artists don't. Even if he or she does, it will likely take years, if not decades. In fact, if you buy based on early promise and notoriety — awards, write-ups, one-man shows, etc. — you may actually be buying at the peak of the market. Thereafter, the value of your newly acquired canvas will only decline or remain stagnant.

Well, okay, you respond. You'll avoid the myriad risks and lousy odds of the contemporary art world and simply purchase art by artists whose reputation has already been clearly established. Surely then, you think, your money is not only safe; a healthy capital gain over time is almost guaranteed. Right?

Wrong. Established artists, too, can go in and out of style. The art world is nothing if not fickle. Thus, the second rule of investing in art: Prices fluctuate according to professional standing. Today's very hot property can be tomorrow's cold reject. Why? Because art, like the hemline, is about fashion. The market constantly needs new artists to stir demand, just as the couturiers of Paris and Milan need new designs each spring and fall. Again, you may think that buying a canvas by the hugely popular Mr. X will insulate you from potential loss. The only thing Mr. X's painting is likely to insulate is your living-room wall. In every other respect, your investment is at the whim and mercy of the mood of the marketplace, which can shift in a nanosecond.

With undiscovered artists, at least you can console yourself with the fact that you acquired the work relatively cheaply. You may be taking a shot in the dark on the artist's future, but your downside risk is limited. When you buy big-name artists, however, your financial exposure is much greater, because you'll have undoubtedly spent a considerable sum to buy the piece. Your upside gain is implicitly limited; your downside risk has increased significantly.

The situation is not vastly different with stock market investments. If you buy 1,000 shares of a penny stock at, say, $1, the most you can lose is $1,000, plus commissions. Even the worst-case scenario is tolerable. And who knows? Maybe the stock tip you got from your brother-in-law's third cousin twice removed will be a high-tech winner, and skyrocket to $50 or more. But if you pay $100 a share for an established blue-chip stock, what are the odds that it will even double or quadruple in price, let alone multiply its value by 50 times? I believe the answer is "infinitesimal".

There's another characteristic associated with the art market that makes it an inferior investment relative to other investments: illiquidity. Illiquidity refers to the difficulty — in terms of cost — with which assets can be purchased and sold. Consider two investments. The cost of selling the first asset is 1% of the asset's value, while the cost of selling the second is 10% of its value. The second asset is more illiquid than the first asset.

The stock market, of course, is significantly more liquid than the art market. That is, on any given business day, it is possible to buy and sell shares in most listed companies. In fact, hundreds of millions of shares change hands every day on world exchanges. And, with the advent of computerized on-line trading, many investors now buy and sell stocks in the same day.

Clearly, the art market is highly illiquid relative to the stock market. Art is typically sold through secretive brokers and auctions, a much less transparent and costlier process than the stock market. This illiquidity effectively reduces the net returns on the art market investment, and is another argument against investing in art. Note that because liquidity is associated with buying and selling, it is a function of the frequency of transactions. Hence, illiquidity is less of a concern for an investor who intends to buy-and-hold, as opposed to an investor expecting to turnover art investments frequently.

You can't do that with paintings. The market is largely illiquid; there are no quick ins and outs. Almost by definition, investing in art calls for a long-term, buy-and-hold strategy. That means your money is effectively tied up, indefinitely, in oil or watercolour or some other medium. If that suits your temperament and your pocketbook, then you may be content to sit back and wait (or pray) for the painting to appreciate. But if you need the money suddenly, you may be forced to sell the work at a loss, because there is no constant demand.

Further, success in the art market, even for established works of art, depends on investors timing their entry into and exit from the market. If you could time the art market with perfect hindsight, you would have done a lot better than indicated in the above table. For example, if you had bought in 1978 and sold in 1990, you would have earned a 12% compound annual return.

But can you really time the art market? How would you know when to buy, or when to sell? While buying in 1978 and selling in 1990 was a successful timing strategy, how would you have known so in 1978?

Further, timing strategies can just as easily be applied to traditional investments, such as bonds or equities. Given the difficulty associated with timing strategies in the first place, and given that timing strategies can be applied to alternative investments that have much higher expected returns and/or lower risk, confidence in timing strategies is a weak argument in favour of art market investments.

The one minor investment attribute that art does seem to posses is that it shares a relatively low correlation with the stock market. Correlation refers to the degree to which the returns associated with two different asset classes move together. High positive correlation suggests that on any given day, if one of the asset classes has positive returns, the other will have positive returns as well. Conversely, high negative correlation suggests that positive returns by one asset class on any given day will be associated with negative returns by the other, and vice versa. Low correlation suggests that returns by one asset class are unrelated to the returns by the other.

Hence, the art market's low correlation with the stock market is good news. The fact that art and stocks don't zig and zag together is good, because it helps to diversify and, hence, reduce the risk of an equity laden portfolio. However, there may be cheaper ways to achieve the desired investment diversification, especially when you take account of the up-to-10% commission incurred whenever you buy or sell a major piece of art.

Now, granted, the above-mentioned researchers did acknowledge that the trifling returns may simply reflect the non-monetary benefits of owning a beautiful piece of art. Indeed, you might sacrifice investment returns in exchange for visual gratification.

From a micro-economic perspective, art investments can be perceived as a combination of investment and consumption. You invest in art hoping it increases (or at least, doesn't decrease) in value. But you also consume art for the pleasure associated with owning art.

The mix of investment and consumption is not exclusive to the art market. Other asset classes exhibit this characteristic as well. For example, consider real estate. Is the purchase of a home an investment or consumption? After all, a home can increase or decrease in value, like any other investment. But a home is also consumed, assuming it is where the homeowner resides. Ultimately, like art, buying a home is both: There are investment and consumption aspects associated with the decision.

To conclude: If you are buying art for both its investment and consumption aspects, it may be a reasonable decision. But, as a pure investment, you and your mutual fund can do better elsewhere.

In sum, keep your Picasso on the wall, and leave him out of your RRSP.

A Money-Back Guarantee on Your Mutual Fund?

3

I'm sure you have noticed that when you buy a stereo, CD player, or fridge, you are usually told that if the product malfunctions — or even if you are not happy with its performance — you can return it for a full, money-back guarantee. Of course, the money-back guarantee is never "free". Even if you are not asked to pay a fee for the guarantee, the fee is hidden in the cost of the product.

Interestingly, many investment and insurance companies offer similar money-back guarantees on mutual funds. If you are unhappy with the performance of your funds — the unit values have declined in price and you have lost money — you can return the units to the vendor and, in many cases, get 100% of your invested money back.

"Wait a minute," you must be saying right about now. "This guarantee sounds too good to be true!" Can it be as easy as returning your units and getting a full refund? It seems suspiciously like the proverbial free lunch. But just like the guarantee you receive when you buy a fridge, the fee for the guarantee must be hidden in the mutual fund, somehow.

So what's the catch?

Well, you are right. There is a catch. You can't return the fund units to the company whenever you want. According to the rules, you must wait 10 years from the date of purchase. If the fund value is under water in 10 years' time, you can go and ask for your money back. But if the fund drops 20% in value two weeks after you purchased the units, don't expect to receive your initial investment back immediately.

Whoa! "Ten years! Why do I have to wait 10 years?" To be technically precise, you can actually get a full money-back guarantee before the 10 years are up — provided you die. Gruesome, but true. Your policy beneficiary can get a refund — even if the account was held for less than 10 years.

Now, having to wait 10 years to trigger the money-back guarantee is irksome. If your investment horizon is less than 10 years — for example, if you intend to roll your mutual fund investments into life annuities in five years, when you turn 65, the money-back guarantee won't help you much.

Further, the probability of actually exercising the right to ask for your money back is quite low. Through quick observation of stock market values over the past 100 years, it is evident that the likelihood of a *diversified portfolio of stocks* being worth less than the initial investment is minimal, although not zero; especially when you focus on narrow indices and markets.

On the other hand, it is always possible that the fund managers associated with a specific mutual fund are inadequate. From this perspective, a money-back guarantee is the way through which the firm managing your mutual funds signals its determination to employ only professional money managers. Through accepting liability for any major "mistakes", the type that could cause fund value to decrease after 10 years, the fund manager will make sure to reduce the likelihood of mistakes in the first place as much as possible.

So here's the main question: Is this investment money-back guarantee of any value? What are the odds that in 10 years — or upon your death — the fund value will be lower than when you bought them?

Surprisingly, this issue seems to be a major point of contention. You'll hear a number of different perspectives, depending on who you ask.

Many financial commentators presume this guarantee is worthless. To them, it's not just a question of value, it's really an issue of fees. You have to pay for this money-back guarantee in the form of higher management fees. For example, you might pay 150 basis points (a basis point is one one-hundredth of a percentage point; so 150 bp is 1.50%) each year in management fees for fund XYZ. But if you buy the money-back guaranteed version, you might pay 250 basis points — which is an additional 100 basis points for the guarantee. Much like the money-back guarantee associated with purchasing a refrigerator, the investor pays for the guarantee.

On the other side of this debate are the insurance companies, their actuaries and the regulators, all of whom are concerned about the potential liability — and stability of the financial system — if the markets were to experience a protracted downturn. If investors are protected from the downside of the market, markets will be more stable. Many of them point to the stock market meltdown in Japan, where market levels are close to 20-year lows.

So what is the catch? Are the higher expenses another attempt to separate you from your hard earned investment returns, or is this a fair payment for the value of a guarantee?

Well, the guarantee certainly has some value. You have to pay — substantially at times — to insure your home, car and life, regardless of how small the pay-out chances are. It is only fair that you pay to insure your investment portfolio.

In fact, this type of guarantee is very similar to another financial product known as a put option, which allows the holder to "put" (read: sell) a stock at a fixed price at some maturity date. For example, you

might purchase a put option that gives you the right
— but not the obligation — to sell 100 shares of Inco
in nine months, for $25 a share. This type of insur-
ance would cost about $2 per share on the Toronto
Stock Exchange. If, in nine months, Inco were trading
for less than $25, you would "exercise your put" and
sell the shares for $25 a share. If Inco is doing
better, you simply discard the (guarantee) put.

So, this money-back investment insurance concept
is not new, it has just been repackaged. In contrast
to a put option, you pay for the money-back guarantee on an ongoing basis in the form of an extra
expense ratio charged to the mutual funds assets. But
when you purchase a mutual fund with a money-back
guarantee, you are actually purchasing a portfolio
consisting of two distinct financial instruments: the
underlying mutual fund, and a put option on the
mutual fund.

With the put option analogy at hand, we can
use some well-established valuation models to get a
rough sense of the fair price for this type of insurance. I analyze these issues in an academic journal article I co-authored (see Milevsky and Posner,
2001).

Table 3 presents our estimates of the fair value
of the guarantee, based on what it would cost the
insurance company to buy put options that protect
your original investment.

Let me explain this table. By up-front cost, I
mean the amount you have to pay out-of-pocket to
acquire the protection. Of course, when you buy such
a mutual fund, you don't pay for the downside protection immediately; you pay annually, in the form
of a higher management expense ratio (MER). Therefore, by "additional MER fees", I mean the additional
amount you would have to pay every year to fund the
guarantee.

TABLE 3

The Fair Value of a 10-Year Money-Back Guarantee,
on a $10,000 Initial Investment

Type of Mutual Fund	Up-Front Cost	Additional MER Fees
Bond Fund	$ 20	2 basis points
Balanced Fund	$130	13 basis points
Equity Growth Fund	$450	45 basis points

For example, if you purchase $10,000 of a Growth Fund — with a money-back guarantee — the downside protection guarantee that you receive is worth about $450. If, instead of paying for the guarantee up-front, which nobody does, you pay in annual instalments in the form of higher MERs, the value is an additional 45 basis points.

Notice that the money-back guarantee is worth much more on the equity fund than it is on the bond fund. The reason for this discrepancy is differences in the volatility associated with each of these funds. Equity funds are much more volatile than bond funds. You need not look much farther than the last two years of capital markets to make that conclusion. While the risk–return tradeoff suggests that the higher risk associated with equity funds results in higher expected return, the volatility also suggests that the probability of losing money on the equity fund is also higher than for the bond fund. After all, what are the odds of losing money in a bond fund — over a 10-year period! It's the volatility that makes the insurance more expensive.

So, if your company is charging *much* more than 45 basis points for the money-back guarantee on an Equity Growth fund, you are probably paying too much. If they are charging *much* less than 45 basis points, you might want to alert the office of the superintendent of financial institutions (OSFI). Finally, if they are charging you in the ballpark of 45 basis points, you have a fair deal and are getting your money's worth. Remember, though the value may be 45 basis points, the security and comfort it provides you might be infinite.

A few things are worth noting about the value of these guarantees. First, the longer it takes to get your money back, the less it is worth. All else being equal, a five-year guarantee is worth more than a 10-year guarantee. Clearly, I would rather get my money back sooner than later. Indeed, some fund companies have recently started offering five-year products with higher associated fees.

Second point worth mentioning is the death benefit I alluded to earlier. Recall that if the fund units drown, the company refunds the original investment in 10 years — or at death — whichever comes first. Therefore, the older (and more male) you are, the greater the chances of death within 10 years — no, not very pleasant to think of — and the greater the value of the guarantee.

This is why the product should rightfully and prudently be recommended to elderly investors — the group that associates with a higher mortality rate — with somewhat shorter time horizons *and* who are very nervous about the downside risk.

I personally — currently in my mid-thirties and a religious apostle of the long-term dominance of corporate equity — have very little need for this type of guarantee, even if it is offered at a very cheap price. (Although it certainly would have been nice to have during the last few years, with perfect hindsight.)

In sum, as with any insurance decision, you must always ask yourself two questions. How much protection do I need? Am I getting a fair price? The above discussion addresses the cost. Only you, however, can determine if you need the protection.

Dollar–Cost Averaging: Emotional Panacea or Logical Fallacy?

Talk to average Canadian investors about their approach to investing, and the expression "dollar-cost averaging" is sure to be mentioned in the first sentence or two. Indeed, it seems as if dollar-cost averaging has become synonymous with the process of investing itself.

For the record, dollar-cost averaging — or DCA for short — is a systematic investment strategy in which a fixed dollar amount is invested on a regular basis in a particular stock or mutual fund. An alternative to the DCA strategy is to invest the entire amount available in the stock or mutual fund immediately.

For example, consider an investor with $6,000 available to invest over the next year. Using a DCA strategy, $500 is invested every month in the same mutual fund, regardless of the value per unit of the fund. The remainder of the $6,000 of available funds is invested in a risk-free GIC or bank account until they are invested in the mutual fund.

According to the innumerable advocates of DCA, this method of investing has the benefit of getting more units when prices are lower, and fewer units when prices are higher. The cheaper the price, the more units you buy; conversely, the more expensive the price, the fewer units you acquire. Lo and behold, at the end of the year you will find that the average cost of the fund units you've purchased is *lower* than the average price of the fund units during the year.

In our example, consider a situation where the value per unit of the mutual fund is $50 in January. In that case, the amount available for investment, $500, is divided by the value per unit, $50, to determine the number of units that are to be purchased. Hence, 10 units are purchased in January. If the value per unit drops to $25 in February, then 20 units are purchased in February, as $500 divided by $25 equals 20. Should the value per unit jump to $100 in March, then five units are purchased in March, as $500 divided by $100 equals five. The number of units purchased in each subsequent month is determined using a similar method.

The average value per unit over the three months is equal to $58.33. But by using the DCA strategy, 35 units are purchased over the three months, costing $1,500, with an average value of $42.86 per unit.

As we see, cost per unit is significantly lower using dollar-cost averaging — and therefore DCA is a superior investment strategy. So goes the steady pitch from financial planners, investment advisors, stockbrokers and, even, mutual fund companies themselves. Buy, continue to buy, and never stop buying. After all, with DCA, you can never go wrong: When prices are high, you buy. When prices are low, you buy. And in both cases, advocates argue, you're doing the right thing!

You may be surprised to learn that many finance professors, such as myself, have decried the inefficiency and outright abuse of this strategy for about as long as DCA has been preached as gospel.

That's right. In my opinion, DCA is *inefficient*, and is not a good idea. Sounds odd? Well, let me try to explain.

You should realize that DCA is essentially a "bearish" bet on the markets. You buy a few units now, in the hope that you will be able to buy even more units when they become cheaper. That boils down to market timing, plain and simple. Why? Because purchasing fewer units when prices are higher suggests that the investor expects prices to go down. Similarly, purchasing more units when prices are lower suggests that the investor expects prices to rise.

But modern finance theory argues that market timing is not a rational investment strategy, as it requires the investor to have premonitions regarding the future values of the asset. While we *can* look back and determine what was the best time to buy and best time to sell assets, in an efficient market where prices quickly and accurately reflect all relevant information, there is no way to determine these times before the fact.

Further, if you truly are confident regarding the future direction of the asset value, why invest *any* money when value is high? After all, if you expect asset values to decrease, why not simply wait until the decrease in value occurs before investing? For example, if you believe that the unit price for a mutual fund you wish to invest in will decrease over the next month, you shouldn't purchase *any* units this month. Similarly, if you expect prices to go up, you should invest as much as possible immediately, and not spread your investment out over time. The suggestion that a fixed amount should be invested in any given month suggests that the investor is unsure about the future, and therefore hesitant. As a timing strategy, DCA is a half-hearted effort.

Proponents of DCA are quick to rebut that investing in the equity markets slowly, as opposed to all at once, reduces volatility. Any reduction in volatility is welcomed, as it reduces the risk associated with the investment strategy.

	TABLE 4	
*Allocated to Fund**	*Expected Wealth*	*Standard Deviation*
$10,000	$11,250	$2,000
$ 7,500	$11,062	$1,500
$ 5,605	$10,920	$1,121
$ 4,942	$10,871	$ 980
$ 2,500	$10,688	$ 500
$ 0	$10,500	$ 0
DCA	$10,871	$1,121

* The remainder — not allocated to the fund — is allocated to the GIC.

Source: M.A. Milevsky and S. Posner, "A Continuous-Time Analysis of the Risks and Rewards from Dollar-Cost Averaging," forthcoming, *International Journal of Theoretical and Applied Finance*, World Scientific Publishing, 2003.

But the truth is the exact opposite. A far more efficient alternative to DCA is to split your money and put half of it into an equity fund *right now* and the other half into a GIC *right now*. In other words, if you have a choice, don't wait to invest.

Table 4 — extracted from a research paper that I wrote with Steven Posner a few years ago — should give you a sense of the reward-and-risk tradeoff from the two different methods of investing. As I will demonstrate, our results clearly show that the DCA strategy does not result in superior returns, even after adjusting for risk.

The table considers a number of investment strategies that an investor with $10,000 may choose. The first six strategies are a variety of immediate investments in a mutual fund, ranging from the entire

$10,000 available to zero. The final strategy is the DCA strategy, where one-twelfth of the available cash is invested in the fund each month. Available cash not allocated to the fund is allocated to the investor's bank account that earns 5%.

In our study, we ask the following questions: What is the investor's expected wealth after one year? And what is the risk associated with each strategy? We measure risk using a statistical measure called *standard deviation*, which is a common measure of asset volatility. The higher the standard deviation, the riskier the strategy.

As displayed in the table, we calculate year-end wealth and standard deviation. For example, if you invest $10,000 in a Canadian equity fund, at year-end you can *expect* — no guarantees — to have $11,250. This is because the long-term appreciation rate of the Canadian equity market has been, roughly, 11.25% per year. There is absolutely no guarantee this will persist. Rather, this is what you *would have* received on *average*.

Of course, equity returns are variable, which means that at year-end, your investment may be in the region of $11,250. The standard deviation value is $2,000. The $2,000 corresponds with a 20% volatility, which is typical of a diversified Canadian equity fund. To be statistically precise, two-thirds of the time your investment will be worth between $9,250 and $13,250 (i.e., $11,250 +/– $2,000) at year-end. One-third of the time, your investment will be either lower or higher than this range.

Now, let's consider the DCA alternative: What happens if you put the money in a savings account and gradually, *slowly*, using the dollar-cost averaging approach, invest your $10,000 into the Canadian equity fund on a monthly basis, one-twelfth at a time?

The table indicates that you can *expect* to have $10,871 at year-end. But in this case, the standard deviation is $1,121. Technically speaking, two-thirds of the time you will have between $9,750 and $11,992, and one-third of the time you will have less than or more than this range of values.

It's difficult to compare these two strategies. While the strategy of investing the entire $10,000 up front results in greater expected wealth, it is also associated with greater standard deviation. Because risk levels are different, comparing these two strategies is like comparing apples and oranges.

But the inefficiency of dollar-cost averaging should become evident through considering the following two strategies: a strategy that results in the same expected wealth at the end of the period, and a strategy that results in the same standard deviation.

Let's first consider a strategy that results in the same expected wealth at the end of the period. As you will notice, from the table, if you allocated $4,942 to the mutual fund, and the remainder to the GIC, you could *expect* to receive the same $10,871 as DCA. Yet, the variability of your investment would be much lower; *plus or minus* $980, versus *plus or minus* $1,121.

This should tell you that you can generate the same expected return as DCA — namely the $10,871 — but with lower risk, by splitting your money roughly in half: one part going into the equity fund, the other going into the GIC.

Let's next consider a strategy that results in the same standard deviation. The table indicates that if you invest $5,605 into the mutual fund, you will have $10,920 at year-end, with a standard deviation of $1,121. This is the same variability as the DCA strategy. But it provides a better return; here, you can *expect* to earn $10,920, which is $49 more than the $10,871 you would have received from DCA.

As the example displayed in the table demonstrates, DCA is an inferior strategy. Alternative strategies result in greater expected wealth for the same level of risk, or identical wealth for lower risk.

In sum. Replacing one major investment decision with many smaller ones does not make the final outcome any safer. Therefore, if you have the money now and you have the choice, it is best to pick an asset allocation that you are comfortable with — and live with it. If you don't have the money now, invest it as soon as it is available, without using an averaging strategy.

One final point worth noting is that if you use DCA as a *saving* strategy, as opposed to an *investment* strategy, then you are essentially investing when you have the money, and forcing yourself to save, which is a good thing. The conscious decision to split your investments over time is the problem.

Saving money on a regular basis is a wonderful idea; unfortunately, investing it isn't!

How Much Should You Pay to Avoid MERs?

5

With the global equity market's pitiful performance during the last few years, individual investors and financial commentators are focusing more attention on the management expense ratios (MERs) we all pay on our mutual funds.

What exactly is an MER?

Roughly speaking, think of the MER as the mark-up you pay when buying retail compared to wholesale. For example, if the underlying investments contained in your mutual fund earn 13% over the year, and the MER is 3%, then you will be credited with a 10% return. Except for minor timing issues, the difference between the gross return earned by the fund manager and the net return credited to your account is the MER.

Now, if our returns earned 13% per year, we may not mind forking 3% over to the fund management. Unfortunately, the sore point is that MER is charged year after year, regardless of the actual performance of the underlying fund. I don't know about you, but I would wince if I had to fork over 3% of my investment in a mutual fund, after the managers of the mutual fund lost, say, 15% of my investment.

The average MER in Canada is about 2.16%, or 216 basis points. Compare this to the 1.44% average MER in the United States, which brings up the question: Do Canadian investors truly receive superior service from their investment managers, to justify the spread between Canadian and U.S. MERs? Or is the Canadian investment management industry simply too concentrated, resulting in higher MERs than the more competitive U.S. investment management industry? The answer to this question is unknown, but is likely a combination of both factors.

Some fund types are associated with higher MERs than others. According to Morningstar, a database of Canadian mutual fund information, currency-oriented specialty funds have the highest average MER in Canada, while money market funds have the lowest. Currency-oriented specialty funds can have MERs as high as 4.75%, while money market funds have MERs of approximately 1% on average. Specialty, Labour Sponsored Venture Capital funds and foreign equity funds tend to have higher MERs, arguably because they are more expensive to manage. Transactions costs in acquiring the underlying securities are higher, and the lack of widespread competition may play a role as well.

However, given the relatively small magnitude of the MER compared to the month-to-month volatility of the financial markets (sometimes up to 15%), it is quite difficult to develop an intuitive sense of the long-term effect of MERs.

What is a fair MER? Are we overpaying MERs?

More important, is it worth the hassle to get out of a high MER fund in exchange for a similar one with a lower MER? Can a tenth of a percentage point amount to much?

Well, here is a thought experiment that should help you in "costing" the MERs to determine if it is worth switching.

Think of two mutual funds, generically labelled as Fund A and Fund B. They both invest in the exact same securities and are essentially mirror images of each other, with one important difference. Fund A is run by a non-profit organization that charges a zero

MER. In contrast, Fund B is managed by a conventional company and, therefore, charges a hefty MER. Clearly, given that both funds hold identical securities, the gross annual returns on the fund will be the same. The net returns will differ, of course. Fund A's net return will equal the gross return, since the MER is zero. Fund B will suffer from an MER drag.

Over time the gap in cumulative returns will get larger and larger. Why? Because every year, investors in Fund A can reinvest an amount equal to the MER that investors in Fund B pay. These additional investments, while small, increase in value due to the power of compounding: not only do these small amounts increase in value, but the increase in value itself increases in value in future periods. The result is that the "small" gap between Fund A and B accumulates into a large gap over the years.

You may think that a zero MER can only be a whimsical figment of my imagination, but in fact, Vanguard in the United States, with its close to eight basis point MER on the S&P 500 index fund, is almost there. Also, basket-like securities, available on the TSE and NYSE, are virtually identical to mutual funds with MERs in the low teens.

Assume you invest $100 in Fund B (high MER), and you plan to hold the fund for 10 years. As an alternative, how much money would you have to invest in Fund A (zero MER), so that you end up with the exact same amount of money after 10 years? Clearly, you need to invest less than $100 in Fund A, to catch up to Fund B in 10 years. But *how much less* do you require up front to match Fund B? Table 5 provides some answers.

Table 5 considers 30 different cases, each one representing a given MER, expressed as basis points, and a given holding period. The MERs range from 20 to 250 basis points, while the holding periods range from one year to 30 years. For each, I present the

TABLE 5

*What Is the Up-Front Price, to Avoid Paying
Annual Expenses?*

	Assumed Holding Period for the $100 Initial Investment				
Annual Expense	*1- Year*	*5- Year*	*10- Year*	*20- Year*	*30- Year*
20 basis points	$0.20	$ 1.00	$ 1.98	$ 3.92	$ 5.82
50 basis points	$0.50	$ 2.47	$ 4.88	$ 9.52	$13.93
100 basis points	$1.00	$ 4.88	$ 9.52	$18.13	$25.92
150 basis points	$1.49	$ 7.23	$13.93	$25.92	$36.24
200 basis points	$1.98	$ 9.52	$18.13	$32.97	$45.12
250 basis points	$2.47	$11.75	$22.12	$39.35	$52.76

Source: Author calculations.

amount you would have to pay today to avoid paying the specified MER over the specified holding period.

For example, the cost of avoiding a mutual fund that charges a 150 basis point MER for the next 20 years is $25.92. This means that you should consider the difference between investing $100 in a mutual fund that charges 150 bp for the next 20 years and investing ($100 – $25.92 =) $74.08 of your money in a mutual fund that charges no MER for the next 20 years insignificant. The difference between the two initial investments can be consumed, or can be invested as well.

This is what I mean by the cost of avoiding an MER. You should be willing to give up more than a quarter of your initial investment, to avoid paying the MER for the next 20 years. In my opinion, this is the true "cost" of an MER.

Indeed, this may seem counter-intuitive at first, so here it goes again. If you invest $100 in a mutual fund that charges a 150 bp MER per annum, you will have the same amount of money after 20 years, compared to a person who invests only $74.08 in a fund that charges no MER — *regardless* of the actual gross investment return from the mutual fund over the next 20 years.

Here is another example, with a more practical way of interpreting the numbers in the table. Suppose you are currently investing in a mutual fund with an MER of 200 basis points. Furthermore, you are planning to hold this fund for the next 10 years. Now, let's say you can locate a fund with similar investment objectives that has an MER of only 100 basis points. According to the table, the savings from switching to this fund would be 100 basis points per year, which translates into ($18.13 – $9.52 =) $8.61 per $100 invested in present value terms. If you have to pay less than $8.61 in loads, fees, commissions and sales charges, it is probably worth the switch. Otherwise, you might as well stay put in the fund that charges the 200 basis points. In most situations, switching should cost much less than 8.61%.

So, in a sense, without passing judgement on fair MERs, the table should give you an indication of how a small "drip" every year can amount to quite a "hole" in your portfolio as time goes on. While the difference between 200 and 100 basis points may seem negligible, $8.61 per $100 invested definitely is not.

You see, I don't mind a 3% MER if the fund manager has beaten his or her peers by three or four times the same MER. But the problem is that so few actually do. (At least, mine never do.)

In fact, here is a suggestion. How about we start paying mutual fund managers based on the performance of their funds, relative to a suitably calibrated benchmark. Executive compensation specialists talk about the importance of aligning management behaviour with shareholder interests. Perhaps it's time to grant fund managers bonuses — or stock options — on the actual unit values or appreciation rates.

For example, a mutual fund can be set up so that if unit values appreciate, investors pay a fee equivalent to 25% of the appreciation to the managers. If unit values decrease, the fund managers pay 25% of the decrease to the investors.

These types of contingent contract are quite common in the exclusive private managed money and hedge fund business, so why not (convince the regulators to) adopt it in the mutual fund business?

Mortality Swaps: A Free Dinner?

6

It doesn't take a Ph.D. in finance to realize that, mathematically, one *minus* one is precisely zero. If you add something, and then subtract it, you should end up exactly where you started. In practice, though, when attempting to undo things — by reversing them — you may be left with much less.

Did you ever buy a stock only to regret it a few seconds later? By the time you reverse the transaction — sell the stock — you probably lost on commissions and the bid/ask spread.

The puzzling fact is that when you try to "do and undo" a particular type of insurance policy, you may end up financially better off than where you started — *after taxes*.

Moreover, this strategy provides an excellent investment opportunity, generating very high pre-tax returns — with absolutely no risk whatsoever. Interestingly, the older you are the better it gets.

Sounds like the proverbial free lunch? Well, the Canadian government serves this free lunch, and the recipe is in the Canadian Income Tax Act. I like to call this a mortality swap. Here is how it works.

If we can abstract for a moment, life insurance companies provide two basic services (products) that are symmetric opposites.

The first is protection against premature death. The basic principle of life insurance is that in exchange for small monthly premium payments — for the rest of your life — the company guarantees a (large) fixed benefit at death. The longer you live, the worse the deal appears. Your insurance company is rooting for you to live longer, as they receive more premiums before you die.

Hence, when you buy life insurance, both you and your insurance company are gambling. You are betting that you will die before the accumulated value of the premiums — including the value of wealth you could have generated through investing the premiums — is worth more than the eventual payoff. Your insurance company is betting that by the time you die, the accumulated value of the premiums and their subsequent growth is greater than the amount they have to pay upon your death.

If you feel uncomfortable betting on your own death, we can look at life insurance as a bet you can't afford not to make. While we hope to live as long as possible, we rationally must be prepared to support our families should harsh reality interfere with our hopes.

Insurance companies also sell another insurance product, where they effectively are betting that you will die early.

This product, called a "life annuity", is protection against living too long. The way life annuities work is as follows: In exchange for one very large payment now, they guarantee a steady — but small — monthly benefit until your demise. With annuities, the longer you live, the better your investment return.

Hence, the longer you live, the greater the payoff you receive for your initial large up-front payment. A holder of a life annuity doesn't only celebrate life as each month passes — the life annuity holder also celebrates the cheque the insurance company must send every month until death.

Your insurance company, on the other hand, gambles that the payments will end early enough to make the contract profitable for them. Hence, your insurance company is rooting for your earlier demise — at least, in the actuarial sense. This is exactly the opposite situation compared to the life insurance case.

For example, the life annuity may involve the following agreement: You pay your insurance company $100,000. In return, the insurance company agrees to pay you $600 every month until you die. Hence, should you live until 108, you will continue to receive the payments every month until then. But should you die one year after initiating the life annuity, your beneficiaries don't receive a further cent related to the $100,000 you invested.

Each contract, life insurance and life annuity, makes sense to acquire when considered on its own. As mentioned earlier, life insurance is crucial to support loved ones who would suffer should you die and your source of income dry up. Traditionally, life insurance is acquired early in the human lifecycle, when the insurance contract holder is working.

Annuities, on the other hand, are typically purchased during the golden years of retirement to protect you. What do I mean by "protect"? The greatest financial fear retirees face is the fear of running out of money before dying. Because it is difficult to forecast exactly how many years into the future we will die — indeed, it's the last thing most of us want to think about — retirees are constantly faced with the nagging question of whether they will run out of money. To eliminate this worry, insurance companies offer life annuities, which promise a steady stream of cash until death, regardless of how long the annuity holder lives.

In essence, the two products are mirror images of each other. For example, with a life annuity, a 65-year-old female might pay $100,000 right now in exchange for $680 a month for the rest of her life. In contrast, life insurance would cost her approximately $220 per month in exchange for $100,000 at death.

Now, here is where things get interesting. While each contract makes sense on its own, consider the following question: Is it ever worthwhile to purchase both? In other words, is it ever worthwhile to place separate bets on living longer, on the one hand, and dying early, on the other?

While the above question may sound like an academic question with little importance in the real world, I will demonstrate that it's a crucial question — and the answer can reap you financial benefits.

Consider an individual who, on the same day, invests $100,000 in a life annuity, and acquires a life insurance contract that pays $100,000 upon death. To pay the life insurance premiums, the individual uses the payments received from the life annuity.

You *might* think that investing $100,000 to buy a life annuity and then using the monthly benefits to fund a life insurance policy with a $100,000 death benefit is pointless. You would probably earn a monthly cash flow that is pretty close to the interest rate you would get on a bond with a face value of $100,000. After all, you are investing $100,000 right now, and are guaranteed to get the same $100,000 back — at some time. When you take expenses, commissions and fees into account, you would be burning money.

However, it turns out that one *minus* one is greater than zero. If you buy a life annuity and then "reverse it" with life insurance, you will end up with a better return — after taxes — than by buying a generic coupon bearing bond.

The exact reason is somewhat complicated — and please don't bake this at home without parental supervision — but the key lies in the way qualified life insurance and life annuities are taxed. They both have a preferential tax treatment, which means that

TABLE 6			
Female Age at Purchase	*Annual Life Insurance Premium*	*Annual Life Annuity Benefit*	*Grossed Up Return Pre-Tax at a Rate of 50%*
65	$2,566	$ 8,112	8.0%
70	$3,566	$ 9,357	8.4%
75	$4,919	$10,812	9.1%
80	$6,654	$13,162	10.9%

Source: Narat Charupat and Moshe Milevsky, "Mortality Swaps and Tax Arbitrage in the Annuity Market," *Journal of Risk and Insurance* 68, 2 (June 2001): 124–47.

you are paying *less tax* relative to other fixed income investments, such as GICs and CSBs. Ergo, when you combine the life insurance and life annuity — what I call a mortality swap — you neutralize the mortality effects, and come out ahead.

Table 6 should give you a feel for the numbers. It displays the approximate annual insurance premiums and annuity payments on a $100,000 policy. The older you are when you set up a mortality swap, the more expensive the insurance premiums, as you are more likely to die earlier. But the annuity payments are greater as well for older investors. Insurance companies pay more to older annuity holders, as they are less likely to live as long as younger annuity holders.

An added bonus is that for many of these insurance policies, if you ever reach the magical age of 100, the policy will be paid in full, and you can stop paying the premium side of the mortality swap.

As you can see, it's not exactly a "free lunch" since you have to be advanced in age to enjoy its benefits, but it certainly qualifies as a "free dinner".

Some caveats are in order. For this to work, first, you have to be healthy enough to qualify for the life insurance coverage and you must know the premium structure before you purchase the annuity. Second, the mortality swap works better if you buy the insurance and annuity joint-and-last-survivor with your spouse. This means that payments and benefits continue until the last survivor's demise. Also, borrowing money to buy the life annuity — and then buying life insurance — will lead to even higher returns on investment. Of course, there are interest payments associated with borrowing that are not incorporated into Table 6 above.

Finally, you also have to make sure to buy the life annuity and the life insurance from two separate insurance companies — separate underwriting, in the insurance jargon — otherwise the Canada Customs and Revenue Agency won't wink, and they'll take back your free supper.

One final note worth mentioning is that the above-described strategy is just one way to use insurance policies to obtain greater after-tax investment returns than traditional (non-insurance) instruments. You might want to look into this further with the help of a qualified insurance salesperson or financial planner.

Cloning with Derivatives

7

You may have recently heard the term "cloning" used in the same sentence as "investing". Don't worry: While the demand for investment professionals is high, the industry is not cloning the most successful fund managers — yet.

Instead, "cloning" refers to a new type of investment vehicle. Financial "rocket scientists" — maybe molecular biologist at heart — have created "clone funds" to pull the wool over Ottawa's eyes.

What are clones? Clones are funds that are 100% RRSP eligible, as they appear to invest in Canadian capital markets. But clone funds make sure to mirror foreign investments through the use of derivative securities, such as futures contracts.

Hence, while clone funds are officially "Canadian", the returns earned on the clone funds are almost identical (the difference would be attributed to financing costs) to the returns you would earn through investing in foreign markets.

Why invest in clones? The answer is diversification. The diversification effect occurs when the number of investments in the portfolio is increased, and these investments are of numerous diverse asset classes. Assets are placed in classes based on a number of factors, such as industry type, asset type — or geographical location.

For example, if the entire portfolio is invested in energy stocks, then the portfolio is highly sensitive to factors that influence the energy industry, such as events in the Middle East, or the weather. This risk can easily be diversified, through investing in other industries as well. If half of the portfolio is invested in the automobile industry, the diversification effect will kick in: the portfolio will be less sensitive to events that impact the energy industry, because these events likely do not impact the automobile industry in the same way. Of course, some events will affect both industries equally. Hence, a truly diversified portfolio is diversified across numerous industries, and across other classes of investments.

Now, a typical RRSP portfolio may be diversified across a number of factors. With that said, government RRSP restrictions on foreign investment limit the diversification effect, effectively forcing Canadians to invest the vast majority of their portfolios in Canadian assets. The thinking behind the government restrictions on foreign investments is to use the RRSP to support Canadian capital markets — arguably an honourable objective. However, individual investors sought to overcome the limitations on their ability to diversify across geographical classes. In response, the Canadian investment industry responded with the creation of clone funds.

Indeed, following the original lead of creative pioneers, many fund companies in Canada now offer "replicas" of their foreign equity funds — yet are considered 100% domestic content for the purpose of RRSPs.

Effectively, while foreign investment restrictions are still "on the books", they do not apply to any Canadian RRSP holder serious about foreign investments. As the Canadian government has not changed the rules regarding RRSPs, more and more Canadians are using clone funds.

But let's take a step back for a moment and ask the question any thinking Canadian is entitled to ask: How can financial alchemy bypass the 30% foreign content restriction placed on RRSPs? Is the money in Canada, or isn't it? Furthermore, if they are using derivatives, how safe is the investment? Does anybody remember Barings Bank, Long-Term Capital Management, Orange County, or Procter and Gamble? These are all well-known entities that used derivatives — and got burned in the process. Are clone funds a shell game? Or are they a reasonable alternative to traditional mutual funds?

Well, first of all, some soothing words for those of you who have jumped in head first. *Derivative* securities are not riskier than traditional stocks and bonds, which are the *primary* securities on which they are based. Investing in conventional securities using derivatives is merely another way of financing the purchase, so to speak.

What is a derivative security? With a bit of creativity, you can think of a derivative security as a novel layaway plan for stocks, bonds and foreign currency at your favourite investment bank.

Inspired by my impeccably dressed sister-in-law, let us imagine for a moment that while window shopping at Holt Renfrew, you identified an exquisite designer suit — on sale for a mere $1,000 — that you intensely covet. However, since you do not really need the suit right now and, in fact, you don't even have the money for it, you decide to go with a new and creative layaway plan. In exchange for a very minor payment, say $25, Holt Renfrew gives you the right — but not necessarily the obligation — to purchase the designer suit (read: stocks, bonds or foreign currency) for the current sale price of $1,000 within the next year. This is a legally binding contract that obligates them to give you the suit any time you want it, in exchange for the $1,000. Of course, if you find an identical suit for less than $1,000 elsewhere, you can walk away — and forfeit your $25 — from the layaway plan. If the suit goes back to regular price, or for that matter gets even more expensive, you can exercise your option and buy it at the guaranteed price of $1,000. Quite intuitively, Holt Renfrew must hold proper inventory for every layaway plan they guarantee, and they can't sell the same suit twice (also known as naked retailing). In the lingo of modern finance, this novel layaway plan is a derivative on the primary designer suit.

What is more, if you are primarily interested in participating in the potential upward movement of the designer suit value — but not necessarily to wear it — you can roll over this layaway plan year after year. Of course, if you don't buy the suit outright, you don't get to wear it, which means that you forfeit any consumption value. But on the other hand, you can keep your $1,000 in the bank, and get interest on the money you didn't spend on the suit.

In the language of derivative markets, the layaway plan described above is called a "call option". A call option is an agreement between two parties, where one party has the right to purchase a specific asset from the second party at a specific price sometime in the future. It's important to note that while one party has a right, and not an obligation, the second party — the one agreeing to sell the asset at the specific price — is obligated to fulfill his or her side of the contract. In return, the second party receives an up-front fee from the first party.

For example, Bob and Susan agree to arrange a call option between the two of them. Bob has the right to purchase 300 shares in Microsoft Corp. stock from Susan in three months for $123, when the current price is $120. At that time, Susan must sell the stock to Bob for $123, regardless of the market price. In return for this right, Bob pays Susan 50 cents per share, or $150. If the stock price increases to $130 in three months, Bob will exercise his option, and purchase the 300 shares for $123 each. Bob can then turn around and sell the stocks on the market for $130, resulting in an immediate profit of (300 × $7 =) $2,100, not including the $150 fee paid to Susan for the right. On the other hand, if the stock price decreases to $100, Bob will not exercise his right, as it would be irrational to purchase the stocks for $123 when they sell on the market for $100. Hence, Bob will lose his up-front fee of $150, but nothing more.

As we see from the above example, the higher the stock price, the greater the payoff from holding the call option. But the payoff can never be less than zero. Figure 1 is a payoff diagram for the call option described in the example. It describes the payoff to Bob for every possible stock price in three months.

Another derivative security, closely related to options, is futures contracts. A futures contract is similar to a call option, insofar as a specific asset, price, and future point in time are specified. However, unlike a call option, neither party has any rights — instead, both are obligated to transact at the specified date, regardless of market price. Since neither party

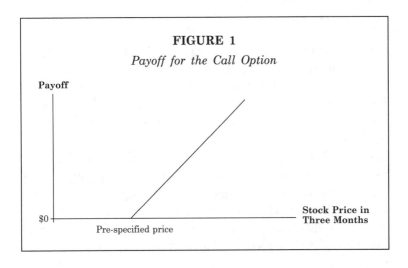

FIGURE 1

Payoff for the Call Option

has superior rights, there is no up-front fee associated with a futures contract at initiation.

To price the up-front fee associated with options, and the pre-specified price associated with futures, we use highly technical calculations, which are beyond the scope of this book.

What does this have to with RRSPs and mutual funds? Well, your friendly neighbourhood mutual fund company is taking your investment contributions and using a very small portion to participate in a souped-up layaway plan — options and futures — on stocks and bonds. These stocks and bonds are the ones that are being held in the underlying fund being cloned. The very minor payments must be made in foreign currency to an investment bank that guarantees the layaway price, but the rest of the money can remain in Canadian treasury bills.

What this essentially means is that although you and your mutual fund personally are holding very little foreign content, some other investment bank is holding the large bulk, since somebody is going to have to deliver that "suit" when the "layaway plan" comes due. Of course, the investment bank does not have any foreign content restrictions.

In my opinion this state of affairs is ridiculous. What is happening now is that Canadians can completely bypass the tax restrictions by using derivatives — which is perfectly legal, I might add — but must pay more for this privilege with higher MERs. The added fees range in the 30 to 60 basis point range. Sure, I would pay to get products with better risk-and-return characteristics, but there is a much better solution. That is, simply abolish the foreign content restriction, since, *de facto*, they no longer exist anyway. And no, we will not experience a massive collapse in the Canadian stock market as money starts to flow out — and what a pessimistic view of the Canadian economy that defence entails.

Risk and Retirement

8

My father-in-law recently retired at age 65. He is thrilled that he doesn't have to work any more since he didn't really care much for his co-workers or his boss. But most of all, he is glad that the stress of day-to-day business life is over. Now he gets quarterly statements from his investment advisor. It seems that his equity portfolio has taken big investment hits in the last while. Talk about stress!

So, he called me up with an often-heard question: "I'm retired now, am I too old for the stock market?"

For many investment advisors, the knee-jerk reaction to such a question is that retirees should completely avoid the stock market, or any other investment that shares its risk characteristics. After all, many would argue, retirees do not have a salaried income that can help them recover should their equity investments take a catastrophic hit. Instead, retirees completely rely on their savings. When those savings are gone — they are gone for good.

Unlike an investor aged 35, who has 30 years before retirement to rehabilitate catastrophic portfolio performance, a retiree will "feel" his or her loss in a very personal way — in terms of lower consumption, and possibly the need to rely on others for financial support. Hence, a compelling argument can be made that retirees should play it safe, stay out of the stock market, and invest their money where it belongs — in low risk, fixed-income securities.

But I beg to differ. My answer to my father-in-law, and to so many others that face this dilemma, is: You probably should be investing in the stock market, with the emphasis on "probably". Completely exiting the stock market at 65 is simply too early.

So, at what age should you declare victory, pack up your mutual funds and flee to the relative safety of fixed-income securities? Well, the odds indicate that it is much later than you think.

Let me start with a concrete example. Suppose you have just retired at age 65 with a small pension and a nest egg of $100,000, which must last for the rest of your life. Let's further assume that, in addition to your small pension, you would like to consume $7,500 per year (after inflation) throughout your retirement. The easiest way to implement this is with a systematic withdrawal plan.

The crucial question is: How should you invest the $100,000 dollars? Should you allocate most of the money to safe short-term GICs and other fixed-income securities, or should you invest in a portfolio of equities and mutual funds?

While you may be focused on the risks associated with the stock market, there are actually two sources of uncertainty that you face. On the one hand, if you invest primarily in equity products and the market takes a serious tumble early in your retirement years, your nest egg will get devastated, and you may not be able to fund the desired consumption. For example, stock market declines of 25% in a single year are not uncommon. Such a decline can seriously damage your savings, and your future.

On the other hand, if you invest primarily in low yielding fixed-income products and you live a long and healthy life, you may not be able to fund the desired consumption either. In other words, you face the risk of outliving your money. For example, if your systematic withdrawal plan is based on the assumption of 20 years between retirement and death, when in fact you live 35 years after retirement, you may face 15 years of impoverishment, at a time when you are unable to generate any income. While we all wish for long life, we face the risk that our money runs out before death.

So which risk is worse? Is the security associated with fixed-income investments an acceptable tradeoff for the risk of outliving your money?

Here is one way to answer this kind of question. The idea is as follows: Some colleagues and I at York University created a computer program that generates millions of different future financial scenarios for the world. It's the ultimate imagination machine. In one scenario you live to a ripe old age of 95, in another scenario you live to age 75. Some scenarios have the stock market booming for the next 20 years, and other scenarios have a 10-year bear market.

Of course, the likelihood of each of the scenarios occurring is not identical. The probability of dying at age 75 is much greater than the probability of dying at age 95. And the probability of the stock market booming for 20 years is very unlikely, as we have all learned from bitter experience. To address differences in likelihood, our computer program generates scenarios based on the likelihood of them occurring. Hence, of the millions of different scenarios we generate, many more are associated with living until the age of 75 rather than 95, or of moderate stock market performance rather than incredible performance or failure.

The probabilities for these human-lifetime scenarios were taken from Statistics Canada mortality tables; the probabilities for the stock market and interest rate evolution were generated using historical statistical estimates. We let the computer run all night, churning out millions of different cases, and then came back in the morning to start counting.

Specifically, for each and every possible asset allocation, we counted the number of times that the 65-year-old, who consumes $7,500 per year, runs out of money *before* he or she dies. These are the people who starve. The remaining people, who die with wealth, have managed to "avoid outliving their money". The probability of outliving your money is equivalent to the number of scenarios where the individual runs out of money before he or she dies, divided by the total number of scenarios.

For example, let's say we run 2 million scenarios, and 1.3 million run out of money before death, while the remaining 0.7 million avoid outliving their money. In this case, we would calculate the probability of running out of money as 1.3 million divided by 2 million, or 65%. But if only 0.2 million of the 2 million run out of money before death, then we would calculate the probability of running out of money as 0.2 million divided by 2 million, or 10%.

Table 7 provides you with some of our results. In this table, we assume that your current age is 65, your wealth at age 65 is $100,000, and the annual level of consumption you wish to sustain is $7,500, after adjusting for inflation.

Table 7 strongly suggests that *not* allocating a significant portion of one's portfolio to the equity market will likely result in you running out of money. For example, if the 65-year-old female allocates all of her $100,000 to short-term GICs, with no exposure to the equity markets, there is a 71% chance that she will not be able to consume the desired $7,500 until death. In other words, there is a 71% chance that she will outlive her money. In contrast, however, the male at the same age who allocates 0% to equities has a lower, 47%, chance of outliving his money. This number is still quite high, but as you probably guessed, it

TABLE 7
*Probability of Outliving Your Money Depending on
Asset Allocation*

Equity Allocation	Male	Female
0%	47%	71%
20%	37%	59%
40%	30%	47%
60%	26%	39%
80%	23%	35%
100%	22%	32%

Note: The remaining wealth, that is not allocated to the equity market, is allocated to short-term GICs.

Source: M.A. Milevsky with C. Robinson, "Self-Annuitization and Ruin in Retirement," *North American Actuarial Journal* 4, 4 (October 2000): 112–29.

is lower than the female's probability, simply because he does not live — and consume — as long.

As the 65-year-old moves into a more aggressive allocation to equity, the probability of outliving wealth decreases. At a 60% allocation to equity, the female has a 39% chance of running out of money, and the male has a 26% chance.

Remember that according to Statistics Canada, a 65-year-old female has a 36% chance of living to age 90, which is 25 years of retirement consumption. A 65-year-old male, on the other hand, has a 38% chance of spending 20 years in retirement. So the odds are, you have a long horizon in the golden years, which leaves plenty of time for equity.

Two final caveats are important at this time, before you rush out and convert your GICs into a mutual fund that invests heavily in NASDAQ equities.

First, while the probability of outliving your money is lower if you allocate a greater proportion of your portfolio to the stock market, there is no guarantee that you are better off investing in the stock market than in fixed-income securities. After all, the stock market may have years of poor returns, resulting in a significant decline in your wealth. Ultimately, allocating investment dollars to the stock market is a gamble: On the one hand, you may lose some of your wealth. On the other hand, your portfolio may grow to the point where your probability of outliving your money is greatly reduced. And, as I have stressed before and will continue to stress, I am talking about broadly diversified portfolios that invest globally and in many different sectors.

Second, remember that insurance companies provide a product that can ensure you won't run out of money before death: life annuities. Of course, this implies forfeiting the capital upon death.

To sum, the conventional wisdom that retirees should avoid the stock market completely and limit their investments to low-risk fixed-income securities should be questioned. For many retirees, investing a portion of the portfolio in risky securities will help them to avoid outliving their money. Younger retirees particularly should have a proportion of their savings invested in equities.

Investing with Other People's Money 9

At first glance, using other people's money in order to invest, also known as leverage, appears quite alluring. Indeed, at times I am quite amazed by the number of otherwise prudent individuals who have thrown caution to the wind and — with apparent brilliant hindsight — have leveraged themselves to phenomenal returns. At other times, I am shocked by the foolishness of people who have caused themselves personal financial difficulties through over-leveraging.

Leveraging is popular among financial "gurus" as well. Over the years, I've reviewed a number of articles and books about "fail safe" investment strategies — apparently using methodologies discovered by the authors, and the authors only — that are simply variations of basic leveraging strategies. As you will likely not be surprised to hear, most of these strategies are not "fail safe", in any sense of the word. Instead, they share the advantages and disadvantages of typical leveraging strategies.

So what exactly is a leveraging strategy? Is leveraging for everyone? And how much leverage should you use?

As a strategy, leveraging is quite simple. First, you borrow money from an entity willing to lend it to you, such as a financial institution or your brother-in-law. Of course, to borrow money, you will likely have to convince the lender that you will be able to repay the loan. Hence, you may have to use the investment, your savings, and/or your home as security. The loan will be for a period of time, such as one year.

Second, you then take the money and use it, in combination with your own cash, to purchase an investment, such as shares in Microsoft or fine art. The value of the investment will either increase or decrease. If the investment value increases over time, you can simply sell the investment, return the borrowed money (plus interest) and pocket your profits. But if the investment goes sour, you'll have to find some way to cover the loan. Hence, you will either have to dip into your savings, plead for an extension on the loan, develop a close and meaningful relationship with your local loan shark, or face personal bankruptcy.

Let me be perfectly clear: A leveraging strategy can be very successful, or it can be a total disaster. In most cases, the result of the strategy will fall somewhere in between. But don't bother with leveraging strategies if you aren't prepared to deal with the aftermath of a disaster.

For example, if you can borrow money at 7% and then invest it at 12% per annum, you can create the perennial money machine. With $1,000 borrowed against $1,000 you already own, the $2,000 in assets translates into $2,240 by year-end. When you pay back the $1,000 plus $70 in interest costs, you are left with $1,170 net, which is a 17% return on your money. Even better, if you borrow $4,000 against the $1,000 you own, the $5,000 in assets grows into $5,600 (12% of $5,000 is $600). Then, after the $4,280 is paid back, the remaining $1,320 is yours to keep, which represents a 32% return; and so on and so forth, with higher amounts of leverage. In fact, if you structure things properly, the interest cost should be tax deductible and the gains mostly capital, which makes leverage even nicer on an after-tax basis.

Of course, the downside occurs when you earn a lot less than what you expected. If, for example in the first case, instead of earning 12% on assets, you lose 12%, the $2,000 deteriorates to $1,760. Then, when you pay back the $1,070 you are left with $690, which is an ugly 31% loss in your equity. You can therefore think of leverage as the investment equivalent of a telescope and microscope built into one. It magnifies the gains and the losses.

Leveraging is apparently a popular strategy in Canada; you probably use this strategy yourself. What do I mean? Well, two of the biggest purchases that a typical Canadian makes during his or her life are a house and a car. Both of these purchases are typically heavily leveraged, whether as a mortgage or a car loan.

Now, when we sign up for a mortgage, we don't think of it in the same way that we think of leverage used to purchase stocks. If we think of it at all, we think of a mortgage or a car loan as a way to spread our expenses over time: we don't have enough money to afford to buy a house or car today, but our human capital — as expressed in the future potential of our paycheques — is sufficient to afford the house or car. Hence, we use the mortgage or car loan to overcome the asymmetry between our immediate need for cash, and the amount of time until we can liquidate our human capital through our paycheques.

But in reality, signing up for a mortgage or a car loan is identical to taking a highly leveraged position to invest in shares of Microsoft. In all three situations, the investor puts down a proportion of the entire cost of the investment, and uses leverage to finance the rest of the cost. By a mortgage or a car loan, the house or the car are used as security against the leverage. By leveraging to purchase stocks, the stocks themselves, retirement savings, or your home are used as security.

	TABLE 8 *What Is the Probability?*		
Leverage	*Nasty Loss* *Return ≤ −15%*	*Typical* *−15% < Return < 30%*	*Huge Win* *30% ≤ Return*
None	0.13	0.59	0.28
50%	0.21	0.42	0.37
100%	0.26	0.32	0.42
400%	0.36	0.13	0.51

Source: Author calculations, log normal distribution, historical mean and variance of diversified equity portfolio.

So, practically speaking — whether you are borrowing against your house or your personal retirement plan — how can you know in advance if the gods of chance will smile on your leveraged portfolio?

Well, Table 8 should give you a good indication of the "probabilistic" effect of leverage. It reports the odds of a variety of investment outcomes, depending on the amount of leverage that you assume.

In the table, I assume that the portfolio grows at 12%, with a variability of +/− 25%, per annum. That is, two-thirds of the time the return will be within the range of −13% and +37%. I also assume that the interest (margin) cost is 7%. Tax considerations are not included in the table but would, actually, make them look better.

I consider four leverage strategies, ranging from no leverage to 400% leverage. A 50% leveraging strategy means that you borrow 50 cents for every dollar of your own that you invest. A 400% leveraging strategy means that you borrow $4 for every dollar invested.

For each strategy, I report the probability of three scenarios occurring, which I label "nasty loss", "typical" and "huge win". The nasty scenario corresponds to returns equal to or less than 15%. The typical scenario corresponds to returns ranging between negative 15% and 30%. The huge win scenario corresponds to returns greater than or equal to 30%. The titles are not very descriptive (what is typical?), but you should get the point.

For example, when you invest in a relatively diversified portfolio of equities, such as a mutual fund, with absolutely no leverage, the probability of losing more than 15% in any given year of your initial investment is 0.13, which is material, but not much. On the favourable side, the probability of earning more than 30% is about 0.28. Logically, the chances of earning an amount that is exactly between minus 15% and 30%, is 0.59. Indeed, the three numbers, 0.13, 0.59 and 0.28, should sum to exactly 1.00, since all outcomes are itemized.

Now let us look at the effect of 100% leverage. Notice that in this case, the probability of earning less than minus 15% is a much higher 0.26, which is double the odds of no leverage. Likewise, the probability of earning more than 30% is a more sizeable 0.42. In the middle, the probability of earning between minus 15% and 30% has been reduced to 0.32, compared to 0.59 with no leverage. As you can see, the rows still add up to 1, but the "mass" is moving towards the tails. In other words, leverage increases the odds of extreme outcomes, both good and bad.

In the final case, with 400% leverage — which, remember, is $4 borrowed for every $1 in equity — the probability of extremes is at its highest. The chances of earning less than minus 15% is a substantial 0.36, and the probability of earning more than 30% is a sizeable 0.51. This is precisely what is meant by the high risk in leverage strategies. The extremes are more likely to occur — and therefore surprises are the norm — compared to the average. Notice how the typical returns become less and less likely as the amount of leverage increases.

So, as you can see, it is somewhat unfortunate that you must take the bad (downside risk) with the good (upside potential). Indeed, this is why most investment houses and regulators prohibit large amounts of leverage at the retail level (large companies seem to be exempt), and for good reason. At high levels of leverage, you face a better than one out of three chance of "nasty" returns.

So how much leverage is appropriate? Ultimately, the decision depends on the amount of risk you are willing to accept. If you like to gamble, and can find someone to lend you 400% leverage, such a strategy may pose a reasonable alternative to, say, betting on the horses. But if you can't afford to lose large amounts of money, be very careful. As the table demonstrates, leveraging increases the probability of failure as well as the probability of success. For those of us who are willing to take some risk but don't wish to gamble our future away, moderate amounts of leverage may be most appropriate. Indeed, a recent study found that modest amounts of leverage could enhance stock portfolio performance in the long run (Domian and Racine, 2002).

Note that there is one way to eliminate — or at least greatly reduce — the chances of a wretched outcome. That is, you can buy a product with upside potential, but that can't lose money. Sounds impossible? Well, investments with money-back guarantees, such as Segregated funds, Index-Linked Notes and Protected Puts, are all products where the "left tail" is eliminated. In other words, for a fee — either implicit or explicit — financial institutions will sell you products that eliminate the probability of "nasty" outcomes occurring.

Of course, there is no guarantee that the return on these products will beat the interest costs that you must pay on your borrowings, but at least the chance of a true catastrophe is eliminated.

In sum, when contemplating leverage, you must be able to afford the interest payments, without having to sell out at the worst possible time. The most important thing to consider is whether you can afford a disaster. If not, a leveraging strategy may not be for you. On the other hand, if you are willing to accept some risk, a moderate leveraging strategy may pay off in the long run.

What Is Financial Risk?

10

Risk and return. My wife complains that she can't have a decent conversation without my mentioning these words at some point. In fact, my seven-year-old daughter recently asked me at the Friday night dinner table, "Daddy, what is risk?" Gees, what happened to "Why is Barney purple?"

But her question is a good one. What *is* financial risk? How do we measure it? For many investors and market observers, financial risk is synonymous with price volatility, market fluctuations, terrifying headlines and day-to-day uncertainty.

The volatility associated with a stock or portfolio can be measured in a number of ways, and there is no accepted universal measure. One popular method is through the use of standard deviation. Standard deviation is a statistical tool that measures the degree to which the stock or portfolio's returns are dispersed. For example, say you have two portfolios. One portfolio earns an average of 0.5% per month, and rarely or never deviates from the 0.5% return in any given month. Another portfolio also earns 0.5% per month, but in any given month, actual returns are quite different than 0.5%. One month's return may be −18%, followed by a return of +10% in the following month. The standard deviation of the second portfolio will be much higher, because its returns are more dispersed.

Another measure of volatility is beta. Beta is a measure of the stock or portfolio's sensitivity to changes in the stock market. A beta of one suggests average sensitivity: in reaction to events that affect financial markets, the stock or portfolio with a beta of one will move in the same direction, and in the same magnitude, as the general stock market. A beta greater than one suggests heightened sensitivity, while a beta less than one suggests a stock or portfolio less sensitive than the stock market.

For bureaucrats, corporate executives, central bankers, elected politicians, hedge funds and even mutual fund managers, market turmoil is also a very risky business. In many cases, their lucrative jobs may be at stake. For professional investment managers, investment decisions are, effectively, gambles. If the return on the investments beats a pre-specified benchmark, the managers are perceived as "successful". If the return on the investments is lower than the benchmark returns, the manager is perceived as a failure, and may lose his or her job.

However, for individuals facing personal financial decisions, I'm not convinced that volatility and fluctuations capture the true measure of financial risk. To me, financial risk is something much more intuitive than some jagged lines generated on a coloured graph.

In my opinion, historical price movements and the statistical measures that are used to analyze them don't accurately send individual investors the correct message regarding risk.

First, many of these measures are difficult for unsophisticated investors to comprehend. While you don't need an MBA to understand what measures such as standard deviation or beta represent, there is a learning curve associated with such risk measures that many investors simply don't have the time or willingness to understand.

Second, individual investors may consider risk measures based on historical prices that are unrepresentative of future risk. Hence, historical risk is often perceived as ancient history, and not a basis upon which to make future investment decisions.

Third, individual investors may make their investment decisions with hubris — exaggerated self-confidence — and not internalize the potential impact risk can have on their financial well-being.

Fourth, traditional measures of risk provide little insight into how the risk associated with investments changes over time. Is the risk associated with the investment under consideration identical, regardless of how long the investor intends to hold onto the investment? Or is risk a function of time? Practical experience suggests that perceptions of risk are related to the investor's holding period. For example, an investor planning to purchase a house in the next six months is unlikely to be investing anything in the NASDAQ index. But an investor who is planning retirement 25 years into the future may be willing to consider riskier investments.

On the basis of these arguments, a compelling case can be made that traditional measures of risk are insufficient. The academic literature is beginning to recognize this insufficiency as well.

Instead, we require a method of quantifying risk that enables investors to understand the very *personal* nature of risk. This measure also needs to permit investors to understand how the risk associated with different investments impacts them in different ways.

I strongly believe that risk should be framed and explained in terms of what I call the Probability of Regret. Financial risk is the probability that you will look back — with 20/20 hindsight — and regret a financial decision you made. In other words, financial risk is measured by the odds that you could have done better by simply going with the safe, risk-free solution.

We all understand regret, and we definitely don't want to make decisions that we will regret. If financial advisors quantify regret for clients, and demonstrate that the probability of regret associated with one investment is different from the probability of regret associated with another, they can assist clients in making sound decisions on the basis of risk.

Another advantage associated with framing risk in terms of regret is that measures of regret explicitly recognize that the nature of risk changes over time. The likelihood of regret is much greater for short-term investments than it is for long-term investments. The recognition of the role of time in the risk–return equation adds a completely new dimension to financial decision making, and provides investors with another tool to use when evaluating risk.

Sounds a bit too abstract? Here is an example. Imagine you've just won the lottery, or received a windfall inheritance of $10,000. You don't really need the money right now, so you decide to invest it.

You call up your financial advisor and ask: "What should I do with the $10,000? Should I put it all into a well-diversified fund? Or should I play it safe and buy a GIC at the local bank?"

Let's examine the all-or-nothing question in greater detail, focusing on the two extreme alternatives. If you "take the plunge" and invest the $10,000 in the stock market, what are the odds that you will regret this decision?

Figure 2 illustrates what I call the time-adjusted "probability of financial regret". While performing the calculations required to develop the figure, I assumed the investor chooses to invest 30% in Canadian markets and 70% internationally (which, after much analysis, is my preferred mix).

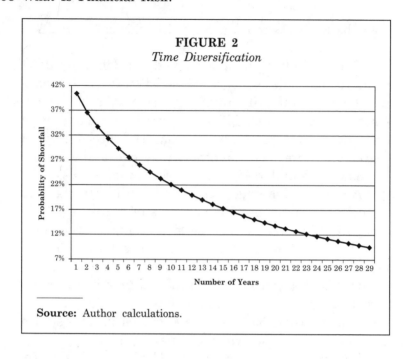

FIGURE 2
Time Diversification

Source: Author calculations.

Given recent capital market experience, it seems that, over a one-year time horizon, there is a 40% chance that a diversified portfolio of equities will underperform the rate of return from the safe bank deposit. Thus, if you're going to need the money in one year, there's a 40% chance that you will regret taking the stock market route. But what if you won't need the money for 10 years? In that case, the figure shows that a diversified portfolio of equities has just a 22% probability of shortfall. Remember, we are not content with just the return of principal. Our regret benchmark is much higher. We want to beat the risk-free investment alternative, which is the bank deposit. Finally, what if your time horizon is 29 years away? In this case, the figure indicates a probability of financial regret of roughly 9.5%.

The important lesson is as follows: As your investment time horizon increases, the probability of regret decreases exponentially. In other words, financial risk has an embedded dimension of time. It is meaningless to talk about whether or not something is risky or safe without addressing the relevant time horizon and the financial alternatives.

Using traditional measures of risk, the answer to this question requires comparison of standard deviations associated with the stock market to the standard deviations of alternative investments. It also requires much debate as to what the investor deems "risky". In the process of answering the question, the individual investor may be left with more questions than when he or she started.

But from the perspective of probability of regret, the answer to the question, "Is the stock market risky?", is: "It depends." Using only a short-term horizon, it's absolutely risky. Using a long-term horizon, I would argue that most equity markets probably are not. Are GICs, treasury bills, Canada Savings Bonds, and term deposits safe? Well, once again, that depends on time. In the short term, they're the safest things available. After all, federal and provincial authorities implicitly guarantee them. Their returns are reliable and predictable. But, in the same manner, I would argue that over the long term, they are the riskiest places for your money because you are likely to outlive your money. In sum, risk is in the time of the beholder.

You must, however, remember one very important thing. Holding a handful of stocks is truly a risky strategy, no matter how long you hold these stocks and no matter how well they seem to have performed in the past. One need look no farther than JDS, Nortel, Enron, Global Crossing, Xerox and WorldCom for examples of widely held and popular stocks that have had spectacular runs, only to come crashing back to earth a few years later. It would have been virtually impossible to predict this just a few years ago, and I'm sure there are many other surprises lurking in the future.

The lesson in all of this is that only a large and well diversified portfolio of stocks can truly grow in the long run. Otherwise, you are simply gambling.

Are You an Active or Passive Investor?

11

Nowadays, there is a great debate among finance professors, such as myself, as to whether or not stock market prices are what is labelled "efficient". On the one side, you have the traditionalists who tend to argue that "markets know best", and the price you see in the daily newspaper, or on your computer screen, is the best measure of a company's worth. These traditionalists are generally sceptical of any attempts to uncover hidden value in the market, and they are downright scornful towards technical analysts. Economists commonly refer to this view as the Efficient Market Hypothesis. The EMH, as it is sometimes known, postulates that markets are efficient in the sense that it is very difficult or even impossible to consistently earn above-average investment returns without taking on excessive levels of risk.

From the perspective of the EMH, it's impossible to second-guess market prices. Markets are never overvalued or undervalued. Instead, the market price reflects the exact price of the underlying equities, in the context of the information currently available regarding the macro-economy, the industry performance, and the performance of individual stocks.

There are actually a number of versions of the EMH, but first some background. The EMH evolved from the Ph.D. of a brilliant finance academic named Eugene Fama in the 1960s. He argued that a market would be efficient when you have a market where numerous parties compete for profits through predicting future values of individual stocks. As well, to be efficient, the parties that trade on the market must be both rational and profit maximizing, and information is freely (or cheaply) available to all participants.

The three versions of the EMH postulated are designated the "weak" form EMH, the "semistrong" form EMH, and the "strong" form EMH.

The weak form EMH states that all historical data, such as past stock prices, is reflected in the current stock price. Hence, regardless of how much time one spends analyzing past stock prices, this information can't be used to profit in the future, as the current price already reflects this information. Hence, the weak form EMH argues that technical analysis, where past stock prices are analyzed like tea leaves, is a complete waste of time. There is strong empirical evidence that both U.S. and Canadian stock markets are weak form efficient.

The semistrong form EMH goes farther than the weak form EMH. It argues that not only is historical data already reflected in the current stock price, but so is all publicly available information. Hence, regardless of how much one analyzes the revenue announcements, changes in management, or analyst reports, this information cannot be used to profit in the future. Hence, the semistrong form EMH argues that fundamental analysis, where all publicly available information is used to predict stock performance, is as much a waste of time as technical analysis.

The strong form EMH goes further than even the semistrong form EMH. It argues that even insider information is fully reflected in stock prices. Hence, as soon as management has a discussion regarding next year's marketing strategy, the implications of the strategy are already reflected in stock prices. Unlike the weak form and semistrong form EMHs, there is no empirical evidence supporting the strong form EMH.

As I discussed, one implication of the EMH is that you can never use publicly available information to make money on the stock market. For example, let's say you are in your favourite deli, and you hear on the blaring TV set that scientists have discovered a way to power automobiles using water. While your immediate reaction would be to dump your oil-based energy stocks and invest in companies that develop energy from water, EMH proponents would strongly suggest you don't bother. By the time you call your broker, the markets will already have adjusted to the new information. Hence, it's too late to dump your oil-based energy stocks, as the price has already dropped. The implication is that you can never make abnormal investment profits using publicly available information, because once information goes public, prices immediately adjust.

But not everyone agrees with the EMH. On the other side of the spectrum, you have the modernists who argue that prices are driven by psychological, sociological, demographic and even marketing factors that have little if anything to do with what a company is really worth. In fact, the extremists among the group of EMH dissidents further argue that if you are smart enough, *you* can actually use publicly available information to consistently outperform the markets.

The concept of using publicly available information to outperform the market may appear both arrogant and irrational. It's arrogant because it implies that an individual investor, using information available to the hundreds of thousands — if not millions — of enthusiastic market followers can somehow discover opportunities that others fail to discover. It's irrational because it implies that countless investors are failing to make decisions that can increase their wealth.

However, EMH dissidents argue that it is, indeed, irrationality that drives market prices to divert from fundamental value, where "fundamental value" is the value of the investment, determined through discounting the expected future cash flows associated with the investment to the present. What causes this irrationality? It's a combination of a sizeable proportion of ignorant traders, herd-like behaviour, and conflicting objectives, such as the need for liquidity.

Ignorant traders are sometimes designated "noise traders", as they create "noise" — diversion from fundamental value — in markets with their faulty buying and selling decisions. Even if there are many market participants who are sophisticated, the noise associated with ignorant traders can cause long-term diversions from fundamental value. The stereotypical ignorant trader is the "day trader", who may engage in numerous daily transactions on the basis of rumour and innuendo, as opposed to a realistic analysis of the facts. In the short term, the sheer ignorance of many traders may become a self-fulfilling prophecy, as their buy or sell orders drive stock values in the direction suggested by the rumour.

It's not difficult to argue that investors, as a class, engage in herd-like behaviour. For example, it's much safer for a mutual fund manager to engage in behaviour similar to other managers than to behave differently. After all, it's much easier to defend an incorrect decision that everyone's made than an incorrect decision no one else made. Imagine explaining to an investor why you were selling Microsoft when everyone else was buying. Contrast this uncomfortable scenario with one where you have to explain to investors why you bought Nortel, when everyone else was buying Nortel. I am sure you'd agree that the investment manager would much rather face the second scenario than the first.

Now, make no mistake about it, this is no academic debate among tweed wearing, pipe-smoking, ivory tower scholars. There are billions of dollars at stake, and both sides have huge fan clubs. Of course, this is not a purely theoretical debate, and evidence is quite readily available for those wishing to argue either perspective. Interestingly, the largest arena where you can watch the action is in the index fund market.

You see, when you compare the performance of actively managed mutual funds — overseen by managers who are bent on beating the market — with the performance of passive index funds managed by simply buying the entire market, it seems that for the most part index funds come out ahead. That's right. You can expect better performance with a passive investment strategy than with an active strategy, even when managed by investment "professionals"!

Table 9 compares the 1-, 5- and 10-year compound annual return for U.S.-based mutual funds and

---

TABLE 9
To Index or Not To Index?

% Returns	1-Year 1998	5-Year 1994–98	10-Year 1989–98
S&P 500 (less 0.9%)	36.8%	26.8%	21.3%
Average U.S. Equity Fund	26.6%	19.7%	16.3%
Difference:	10.2%	7.1%	5.0%

Source: T. Cadsby, *The Power of Index Funds* (Toronto: Stoddart Publishing, 2000).

the S&P 500 index. (The S&P 500 index has 0.9% removed from its performance, in lieu of management costs, to put the comparison on equal footing.) While the numbers are somewhat dated, the message is clear.

While the average U.S. equity mutual fund earned 26.6% during the year 1998, the S&P 500 index earned 36.8%. Likewise, over a 5-year period, the average U.S. equity fund earned 19.7%, while the S&P 500 index earned 26.8%. The same general results apply in the Canadian market as well. It is a fact that even when you account for transaction costs, fees, and commissions, the typical fund manager still underperforms the stock market averages.

Note, however, that these results are more reliable during bull markets, when prices increase, than bear markets, when prices decrease. The cash that most funds hold to prepare for redemptions play a large role.

This is very different from professional sports, where any athlete in major league baseball, for example, can hit, run, and throw better than I could ever hope to. Indeed, it appears that this country is replete with many professional fund managers, analysts, stockbrokers, and traders who simply can't — or don't — do better than your ordinary Joe who picks a collection of random stocks from the Toronto Stock Exchange and other international markets. In no other professional association can you find so many members who fail to display the basic skills on which the association is founded. To add insult to injury, you've probably heard tales of young children — and even monkeys — who beat professional investment managers in the stock picking game!

So, the big question is: What's going on here? Why do so many managers fail to outperform the passive indexes? After all, would a plumber remain in business if he only fixed your leaky faucet 40% of the time? Would a taxi driver remain employed if she got you to your destination only 55% of the time?

Well, the reason for this is quite simple: The members of this association — principally, stock analysts — are competing fiercely to locate hidden and undervalued investments. The one who succeeds must succeed at the expense of all the others, who failed to locate the same undervalued investment. The one who gets there first must win at the expense of all the others, who were too slow out of the gate. Now, as the number of active stock analysts increases, and the number of mutual funds expands, the odds of this happening — consistently, I might add — will continue to decline. This fact goes a long way towards explaining the growth of such passively managed investment products as index funds and exchange traded index units (i60s), which are available on the Toronto Stock Exchange and have a simple mandate to match or replicate the market average. With the odds of successful out-performance continuing to decline, many investors feel that if you can't beat 'em, join 'em. Ironically, in the very long term, if too many investors become disillusioned and shift their investment wealth to index funds that simply mimic the broader indices, there will be fewer analysts actively searching for value, and the possibility of out-performance — or of finding neglected values — will once again increase.

So, what side of the EMH debate am I on? Well, although I readily acknowledge the importance of investor psychology in moving market prices, for the most part, I have yet to find a fail-proof system that can exploit these minor inefficiencies. So, for the meantime, I'm still in the EMH camp, but I'll keep you posted as the evidence continues to roll in.

Taxing Matters

12

Once the annual tax season is behind us, most of us anxiously await the assessment notice from the Canada Customs and Revenue Agency. This procedure always reminds me of waiting for my high school trigonometry homework to be graded. We all heave a collective sigh of relief when Canada Customs and Revenue Agency finally agrees — and better yet, gives us our refund — so that we can file away copies of our tax return for good. Ah, but if things don't go our way, we may be spending a good portion of our summer preparing for a dreaded audit. If only we knew in advance who and what the Canada Customs and Revenue Agency was going to target.

Interestingly, in 1995, the U.S. state of Minnesota — via its department of revenue and with the help of some local Economics professors — conducted a very interesting (and perhaps cruel) experiment. A few months before the local tax-filing deadline, they sent letters to a large group of randomly selected taxpayers informing them their returns would be closely scrutinized and audited by the local authorities. These cheerful letters were received by taxpayers one or two weeks after the Christmas holidays, which was three months before their tax returns were due, but just after the previous fiscal year was completed. So, naturally, the opportunity to engage in any legitimate tax planning was limited. The purpose of this experiment was to gauge the magnitude of actual tax evasion by comparing the randomly targeted returns against other tax filers in the same occupational category as well as against their tax returns in previous years. Note: There were no placebos in this experiment. If you got the letter, you were on the hook.

So, what would you do if you got such a New Year's greeting? While it's never fun getting scrutinized by the tax authorities, one can argue that it's much better to receive a warning regarding potential scrutiny before the fact than after the fact. The warning regarding scrutiny definitely reduces the *moral hazard* associated with filing tax returns. Moral hazard refers to the very human characteristic of behaving recklessly when we don't think anyone is observing our behaviour, and when we don't expect to incur the costs associated with the reckless behaviour.

A classic example of moral hazard is with automobile insurance, where an individual may drive more recklessly knowing that the insurance company can't observe the behaviour, and knowing that most of the costs that may be incurred due to the behaviour will be covered by the automobile insurance policy.

Similarly, we all face moral hazard when filing our tax returns. We may choose to include questionable expenses, or bend the rules in innumerable ways. We don't expect to incur the costs associated with this behaviour, because we don't expect our tax returns to receive the scrutiny they require to catch our manipulations.

Of course, we must ultimately ask ourselves whether our behaviour when filing tax returns is fully ethical. While attempting to reduce taxes within the acceptable boundaries of the tax code is legitimate, some behaviour is not. Although we may individually feel that our tax burden is quite unfair, a greater

TABLE 10
Average Reported Federal Tax

Category	Change from Previous Year
Low Income (< $10,000)	12.0%
Middle Income (< $100,000)	3.4%
High Income (> $100,000)	−6.0%

Source: M. Blumenthal, C. Christian and J. Slemrod, "The Determinants of Income Tax Compliance: Evidence from a Controlled Experiment in Minnesota," NBER Working Paper #6575.

burden falls on our fellow taxpayers when we reduce our taxes unethically.

Back to the story, and notwithstanding the above lecture on ethics, I certainly would be much more careful with any deductions or credits that I claim should I receive warning that my tax returns will be intensely scrutinized. And indeed, that is what happened for the most part in the Minnesota experiment, with one interesting exception. As you can see from Table 10, targeted individuals in the low income category (as defined by the study) reported an average increase of 12.2% in their federal tax payable over the previous year. Likewise, individuals in the middle income category increased their federal tax payable by 3.4%. Please note that these numbers were adjusted for a variety of factors such as inflation and natural wage increases. So the year over year comparison is meaningful.

These increases in taxes make sense, as they suggest that individuals expecting to receive special scrutiny are extra "honest" when filing their taxes. However, the study discovered an interesting inconsistency. Curiously, individuals in the high-income category who received this letter filed a more aggressive tax return. For high-income earners, taxes decreased by 6%! It seems that high-income earners claimed more deductions, used more tax credits and reported markedly lower incomes than in the past year.

At first glance, this sounds crazy. Why would they be more aggressive — on average — if they knew with absolute certainty that they would be audited? Is this simply a statistical anomaly?

Well, a variety of theories have been proposed to explain the perverse high-income result of the infamous "Minnesota Experiment of 1995". An interesting argument goes like this. A tax audit is a bit like buying a vase at a Middle Eastern bazaar (although less pleasant). There is a lot of haggling involved until the final "price" is reached. The buyer starts with a much lower price than what they expect to pay, or even think it is worth. The seller begins with a much higher number. The negotiating procedure converges to some mid-point, based on both parties' aggressiveness and acumen.

Likewise, in our context, the high-income tax filers start the tax reporting process with a "low bid". Clearly, though, the high-income filers expect to pay more than their initial "bid" once the negotiating process is completed. They expect the auditors to reply to their initial bid with a counter bid of their own. This process will bounce back and forth until an exact figure is reached.

For example, according to this argument, a high-income earner may file taxes, claiming to owe $30,000 taxes. The tax authorities reply with their disputed assessment of $40,000. Like a Middle Eastern bazaar, the actual tax liability will be somewhere in between these two figures.

There is an obvious difficulty associated with this explanation: Why should this effect only occur with high-income earners? It's unreasonable to argue that high-income earners are more careful simply because they have larger amounts at stake. While the absolute dollars at risk are definitely greater for high-income earners, the relative dollars at risk — defined as the percentage of total income at risk — is similar for both groups. Indeed, it's reasonable to argue that $3,000 is more precious to an individual earning $90,000 than $30,000 is to an individual earning $900,000.

Is it reasonable to argue that low- or middle-income earners are incapable of participating in the bargaining process? This explanation seems unlikely. There are enough smart people — including finance professors! — firmly implanted in the middle class to make any distinction between the two income categories difficult.

Of course, one may argue that high-income earners are able to purchase a higher quality tax preparation team — consisting of lawyers and accountants — than low- or middle-income earners. The tax team, only affordable to high-income earners, may have superior bargaining capabilities when dealing with the tax authorities.

But this argument is flawed. If high-income earners can purchase high quality tax preparation talent, why would they only do so when faced with scrutiny? Shouldn't their taxes always be reduced by the tax team, not simply when warned about scrutiny?

But the finding that some high-income earners may file lower taxes when faced with scrutiny can be explained as follows: The audit letter induces high-income taxpayers to seek professional help in preparing their return. In other words, high-income taxpayers run to their tax team to deal with the increased scrutiny before the fact, when they typically would not. In the process of preparing for the additional scrutiny, the tax team uncovers legitimate reduction techniques. Hence, the increased scrutiny has a contrarian effect: instead of increasing tax revenues, it may decrease tax revenues collected from high-income earners. Middle- and low-income individuals can't afford the high priced tax team, and therefore do not go through the process of discovering they may owe *less* tax rather than more.

In either event, the effect is the same.

So, being that Minnesota is (cold, and) close enough to Canada, what are the lessons for us all? I believe we can extrapolate the following for Ottawa and the folks at the Canada Customs and Revenue Agency.

First, if Ottawa wants to try the Minnesota experiment — let's call it the Manitoba experiment — don't expect it to necessarily increase the Government of Canada's tax revenue, especially when you account for the expense of running this program. Instead, expect some revenue to increase: revenue from low- and middle-income earners. At the same time, expect some revenue to decrease: revenue from high-income earners.

Second, if you want to increase net tax revenue, use the following strategy: Send the early-warning notices to individuals in the low-to-middle income tax bracket exclusively. Don't warn any of the rich, however. Instead, if you plan to audit the rich, tell them long after they have filed their return. To high-income earners, bad news may be good for their financial health, if it comes early enough.

Insurance: When and Why

13

"Don't take a chance", screams the latest piece of junk mail in my hand. "For only three dollars per week, you can rest assured that you and your loved ones will be fully protected."

Three dollars doesn't sound like much, relative to a noble cause such as protecting your loved ones! Surely you would have to be heartless not to protect your family for only a few dollars a day.

In reality, however, we can't buy insurance for emotional reasons. Instead, careful analysis of exactly why we need insurance is required. Such analysis will help us avoid making foolish insurance decisions — either buying too much, or too little — and will allow us to calibrate exactly how much insurance we need at every stage of our lives.

It seems to me that lately we have been inundated with offers to buy new insurance policies against everything from bad weather on our next vacation to veterinarian care for our next house-pet. In fact, you name the calamity, either imaginary or real, and I bet you that some insurance company is willing to take that risk right off your shaky hands.

With the relatively minor sounding premiums — "less than a coffee a day" — how does a rational consumer go about deciding what to insure and what to ignore? The distress factor is very one sided. If something goes wrong, you will certainly regret not having the insurance. But if nothing happens, all that you forfeit are the few dollars.

The constant stream of advertising leaves many individuals bewildered and confused. After all, you face a number of financial risks. The most dramatic is the risk of dying prematurely and leaving your family destitute. Less dramatic, but equally risky, is becoming disabled to the point where you are unable to work. In some ways, disability is more financially burdensome than death, as not only does your family have to fend for themselves without your income, they must also provide care for you as you recover.

You also face risks every time you drive your car. Indeed, the potential financial damage you can cause with a driving accident is so great that most governments force drivers to purchase automobile insurance. Besides life, disability and automobile risks, you face many other risks as well, such as the risk of your home being destroyed by fire, or of being sued for a vicious cross check against an opponent during a game of hockey.

With the vast array of risks we face, it's no wonder that many individuals don't know how to react when faced with the insurance industry's advertising onslaught.

So which risks should you insure? Which risks are acceptable, and don't require insurance?

Well, as I discuss in my book *Insurance Logic*, it all comes down to why you buy insurance (see Milevsky and Gottesman, 2002). In my mind, there are three types of insurance: insurance for consumption, for investment, and for protection.

The "insurance for consumption" buyer is looking for peace of mind. To him, insurance is about tranquillity, like a soothing herbal tea or back massage; the insurance is being consumed. Hence, the decision to purchase insurance is not made on the basis of the cost of the policy, or on the basis of the potential expenses should the crisis for which the insurance is purchased occur. Instead, insurance is purchased to remove the nagging worry — *any* nagging worry — associated with facing risk. Such an individual will purchase insurance for anything.

The "insurance for investment" buyer perceives insurance as an investment: the monthly premiums are paid to the insurance company in return for the payoff from the insurance company at some unknown point in the future. Hence, in a morbid fashion, the individual who purchases insurance for investment is almost "looking forward" to a crisis occurring, as the crisis will result in the payoff, and will justify the investment. As I will discuss shortly, such an individual is gravely mistaken — and may be the type who justifies money spent in a casino as "investing".

In contrast, the "insurance for protection" buyer looks at the purchase from a more rational risk management perspective. The buyer knows it is not a good investment, per se, but if the protection is important and critical, he or she is willing to pay the price. Hence, protection is only purchased when it is necessary. While each individual defines "necessary" in his or her own way, it's fair to say that if you can afford to cover the loss associated with the crisis on your own, then the insurance is unnecessary. For example, for most of us there is no need to insure against a potential loss of a $50 answering machine, as a $50 loss is not difficult to cover.

Since a lower deductible increases the price of the insurance, an individual who purchases insurance as protection should make the deductible equal to the amount he or she can afford without insurance. Remember, deductible is equivalent to the amount that does not require protection.

In my opinion, the only rational reason to purchase insurance is as protection — and not as consumption or investment.

But why isn't insurance a good investment? Let's consider a situation where an individual purchases more life insurance than is required to sustain his family at the quality of life they currently live. In this case, should the policyholder ever die, the beneficiaries will be multimillionaires. Clearly, this individual is not purchasing insurance as protection for his family against death. Instead, he is "investing" (or speculating) the premiums, with the expectation that it will pay off a huge return should he die during the term of the policy.

Now, besides the impact such a large policy may have on the policyholder's beneficiaries — we'll assume none of them will become motivated to facilitate an early return on investment — I would strongly dissuade you from over-insuring yourself. It's not that there is anything wrong with allowing your family to live a life of luxury should you die. My issue with over-insuring is that there's a good chance that your return on investment will be lower than it would be if you had simply invested the premiums in a mutual fund.

To explain, note that while the potential payoff from over-insuring is quite high, the *expected* payoff is not. After all, you may not die during the term of the life insurance policy, or may die after paying premiums for decades. This is obviously good news for you, the policyholder, but not such good news for the beneficiaries, at least from a financial perspective. Of course, you might get "lucky", and die shortly after initiating the policy, in which case your beneficiaries receive a large payoff, with only a few premiums paid. Since we don't know which scenario will actually occur, the expected return is moderate.

More important than the above consideration, however, are other "frictions" associated with over-insuring versus investing. Insurance policies come with heavy transaction costs, in terms of marketing, management, and fees. Further, insurance policies are highly illiquid. In many cases, should you stop paying the premiums, you are left with nothing. Most crucial, however, is the *adverse selection* issue associated with insurance policies. Adverse selection refers to the tendency for riskier individuals to purchase insurance in greater number than less risky individuals. For example, for an individual who somehow knows that he will die in three years — such as an individual who privately knows that he or she is in bad health — life insurance is a great investment.

Because of adverse selection, insurance companies must charge more for their insurance policies than they would otherwise. Hence, insurance is costlier than it would be otherwise.

So, if you are in the "consumption" or "investment" groups, there is little I can suggest in terms of logical decision making. Purchases boil down to marketing and vulnerability. Good luck, and I hope you are not on too many mailing lists. But if you are in the "protection" group — and want to make a rational decision — I believe you should focus on two things. First you should ask yourself, what is the probability of the ill-fated event occurring? And second, what is the relative magnitude of the financial loss, if indeed it happens? If the answer to the former question is "very small", *and* the answer to the latter question is "very big", then, by all means, buy the insurance. Otherwise, stay away.

Let me explain with an example. Think of a standard (10-year term) life insurance policy. The way it works is that you pay a relatively small monthly premium in exchange for a very large payment — to your beneficiary or estate — in the event of death.

TABLE 11
*What Is the Probability of Dying During
the Next 10 Years?*

Current Age	Female	Male
30	0.50%	0.90%
40	1.00%	3.00%
50	3.00%	6.00%
60	9.00%	16.00%
70	22.00%	35.00%
80	50.00%	66.00%

Source: M.A. Milevsky and A. Gottesman, *Insurance Logic*
(Stoddart, 2002) based on Statistics Canada numbers, 1996.

Now, as you can see from Table 11, the probability of dying during the next 10 years is roughly 70 to 100 times higher at age 80, compared to age 30. Does that mean 80-year-olds should buy more life insurance, since they are more likely to die? Absolutely not. The probability may be higher, but the magnitude of financial loss is much lower. If you die during your 30s, 40s or 50s, your family loses many years of your human capital (read: future lifetime earnings). The relative magnitude of this financial loss can be enormous and devastating. But once you are in your 70s and 80s, the financial value of your future wages and income is greatly reduced. Therefore, the relative magnitude of loss is much lower as well. So you have to balance the two factors: the probability and the magnitude. These are the critical ingredients of prudent insurance. Early in life the probability of loss is small, but the relative magnitude of loss is large.

So what is the lesson for all insurance policies? Remember, no product is sold at cost, or zero profit.

In fact, your premiums are much higher than what the company is expected to pay out, since they are obviously in the business of generating returns for their shareholders.

Personal risk management is about protecting you and your loved ones against unsustainable financial losses. In other words, despite the costs, you and your family benefit in the long run. Consequently, most of these nickel and dime policies that are meant to cover relatively small financial losses are most likely a waste of good premium money. On the other hand, if to you it is simply another type of herbal tea, then by all means, lean back and enjoy.

The Next Big Thing in Wealth Management

14

I'm repeatedly asked by individuals and practitioners across the country what the next *big* thing is going to be in the field of wealth management. Apparently, "futuristic gurus" are predicting inevitable upheaval in all aspects of our personal lives. So it is only fitting that wealth management experience a cataclysmic change as well. Of course, being that my crystal ball has never really functioned properly — and having failed to acquire the ability to prophesy — I usually shy away from telling people about the "end of their days". Indeed, as one well-known (and quite cynical) forecaster used to say: "If you must predict, do it often." This way you should be right every once in a while.

But lately it seems that professional wealth management has been experiencing a revolution of sorts. This is especially true south of the border, where financial trends manifest themselves a few years earlier than they do here.

I am talking, of course, about the exciting development of financial Monte Carlo simulations and computer generated personal money management, or what I like to refer to as weathering and stress testing your financial portfolio.

Stress testing may bring to mind an airplane engineer jumping up and down on the wing of an airplane she just built to make sure it can withstand the stress. Or maybe the time your cardiologist forced you to jog on a machine for 20 minutes to stress test your heart. But you can also stress test your financial portfolio to make sure it can withstand abnormally bad events or bear markets. For example, if the market loses 20% per year for the next five years, will you have to forget about retiring early? What if the energy sector does well, but high-tech plummets? What will your portfolio performance be like in this case? How will your wealth change if you lose your job? If you fail to get a raise for the next 20 years? If you get married? If you get divorced?

In my opinion, there is something fundamentally sensible associated with stress testing your financial portfolio. You wouldn't buy a house that hasn't been inspected, or fly on an airplane that hasn't been rigorously stress tested. If your financial portfolio is being used to fund your retirement — a period of time when you will likely be physically unable to generate alternative sources of income — surely you should test its vulnerability to stressful financial periods?

It all started approximately 10 years ago, with an academic article entitled "Individual versus Institutional Investing" (*Financial Services Review* 1 (1991)), written by the renowned Dr. Harry Markowitz, a Nobel laureate in Economics and one of the founders of modern finance theory. In this article, Dr. Markowitz described the future of personal financial planning, using what he called the Game of Life Simulation. In his vision of the not-too-distant future, individuals would be able to simulate their future lifetime, and measure the financial impact of critical decisions they make today. Think of it as the ultimate imagination machine.

The simulation would consider millions of scenarios. For example, a simulation game could include numerous wage increase and time of death scenarios. In one scenario, you receive a raise of 5% every year, and die at the age of 74. In another scenario, you never receive a raise at all, and die at the age of 124. Of course, every scenario is not given equal weight — you are, unfortunately, much more likely to die at the age of 74 than at the age of 124. Instead, those scenarios that are more likely to occur are more heavily weighted, to provide a final analysis that is a fair estimate of what the future may hold. The weights can be based on historical probabilities and personal family history.

Indeed, the computer technology to generate your financial future is still in its infancy, but there are strong similarities with the science — albeit imprecise at times — of accurate weather forecasting.

You may recall many years ago, your local weather outlook consisted of a simple categorical prediction of whether it would be sunny, cloudy, rainy, or snowy. Statements such as "today it will rain", "tomorrow will be sunny", or "Thursday morning it will snow" were as sophisticated as the reports ever became. Of course, most weather forecasters got it wrong, and the art of weather prediction never garnered much respect.

Then, in the mid-1980s, things started to change. Hand in hand with the development of modern computer technology and the success of the scientific method, the art of weather prediction matured into the science of weather forecasting. Now, you can turn on the weather channel in the morning to learn about a given day's probability of precipitation (PoP). Weather forecasters and their computers use what they know about the science of meteorology to convert today's temperature, humidity and atmospheric pressure into tomorrow's probability of rain. You then take the PoP they compute, and make your decisions accordingly.

As such, weather forecasters now have more flexibility. They don't have to make definitive predictions, which almost always end up being wrong. Instead, they can focus on the probability. Hence, if today's PoP is 40% or higher, you would probably carry an umbrella. If the PoP is lower than 40%, you'd probably leave the rain gear at home, etc.

In the not too distant future, I believe the same approach will be used in financial planning as well. You will be able to simulate the future of your financial portfolio — broadly defined — to obtain probabilities of financial success. The software program will compute the probability that you will achieve your retirement goals; or that you will have enough money to last for the rest of your life; or that you will be able to afford to send your children to university. As such, financial planners — the equivalent of weather forecasters — will no longer be limited by one-dimensional definitive predictions. Like any good bookie, they will simply give you the odds.

Managed Money's Catch 22: Juiced Returns and Stale Prices

15

As you might be aware, Canadian regulators have come down quite hard on the mutual fund and pension managers who manipulated stock prices to inflate their return on investments.

But, amidst the hysteria and fears of foul play, few people realize that all of this activity can actually go both ways. You see, whenever small-cap and illiquid stocks are involved, individual investors can increase their fund returns artificially, beyond the actual return of the stocks that make up the funds.

In other words, it's not only fund managers who are "juicing" returns. Individual investors can juice their fund returns as well. In some sense, the motto is "juice or be juiced".

To many of you, the thought that an individual investor can somehow artificially increase returns may sound crazy. It may not be that unthinkable when a professional manager cooks the books. But what power does an individual investor have to manipulate returns?

Well, think of the following hypothetical scenario. Imagine a mid-cap mutual fund that is holding a variety of illiquid stocks that trade infrequently. Illiquidity refers to the costs associated with transacting stocks. If the cost of transacting one stock is 0.5% of its value, while the cost of transacting a second stock is 2% of its value, the second stock is more illiquid. Liquidity is often measured using the bid–ask spread associated with the stock. The bid–ask spread is the spread between the price buyers bid for the stock, and the price sellers ask for. To purchase the stock immediately, an investor has to be willing to pay the bid–ask spread. The larger the bid–ask spread, the greater the illiquidity.

How does illiquidity enable individual investors to manipulate returns? Before we begin, we must first recognize that there is more than a single answer to the question, "What is the stock's value?" On the one hand, we can argue that the stock's value is the value of its last trade. On the other hand, we can argue that the stock's value is the price we would receive for it should we sell it immediately.

Superficially, it may appear more reasonable to use the value of last trade. First, we know the exact price associated with the previous transaction. Second, we have no information regarding the accurate price right now. Therefore, we have no basis upon which to value the hypothetical transaction.

But there are difficulties associated with determining stock value using its last transaction price. Specifically, the value of the stock may change since the last transaction. These changes in value are not recorded in any transaction. But a strong argument can be made that the price at which the stock would sell today is much more accurate than the price associated with the last trade.

As we see from the above discussion, there is no single "truth" when it comes to stock valuation. A sophisticated investor can take advantage of this lack of "truth" to manipulate returns.

To explain, consider a mutual fund that is holding a few hundred thousand shares of ILQ, a fictitious biotech company. This company has a very small public float and last traded today, at around 11:00 am for a price of $5.00 per share. Currently, it is very close to 4:00 pm, and the stock has not traded

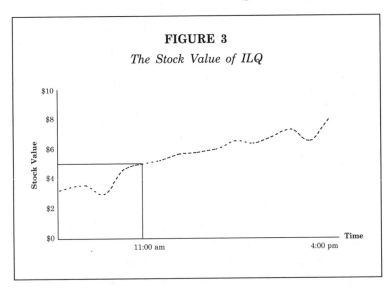

FIGURE 3

The Stock Value of ILQ

in the last five hours. At the same time, the rest of the market has been moving up strongly towards the close. In fact, the biotech indices are all up on the day.

Figure 3 illustrates the scenario described in the example. The broken line represents the actual value of the stock during the day. At 11:00 am, the value of the stock is $5.00. While no further trades take place during the rest of the day, the value has clearly drifted upwards due to the overall upward trend of the market.

Now here is the problem that worries the fund industry. Obviously, if ILQ stock trades again today, prior to the closing bell, it will change hands for more than $5.00. After all, if the market is moving up, then so will ILQ when it eventually trades. The $5.00 "last trade" is therefore known as a "stale price". But then again, if nobody happens to buy (or sell) ILQ before the close of trading for the day, the stock will be settled, or valued, at an artificially low price of $5.00. Any mutual fund that owns ILQ will be considered, from a Net Asset Value (NAV) point of view, to own a stock that is worth exactly $5.00 per share.

So, "Who cares?" you asked. Won't this all clear up tomorrow when the stock does finally trade and its price gets adjusted?

Well, anybody who buys into the above mutual fund at the closing Net Asset Value (NAV) will effectively be acquiring ILQ at an artificially low price. They will be buying into the stock at $5.00 per share. Even though ILQ is clearly worth more than $5.00 per share. Existing unit holders and fund managers are powerless to stop the flow of bargain hunters buying a dollar for 97 cents, or the "option" to buy a mutual fund unit for less than it is really worth.

This, you will notice, is the symmetric opposite of the so-called "juicing", or high closing, problem. In fact, if the fund manager deliberately tries to trade at or about 4:00 pm, to move the last quoted number closer to fair value, they will stand accused of price manipulation.

So, the fund manager is damned if they do, and damned if they don't. And the individual inves-tor can take advantage of the fund manager's dilem-ma through buying into the fund when he or she estimates that prices have risen above the previous transaction price.

Now, this problem may sound a bit esoteric and farfetched; after all, who would be able to keep track of these mispricings? But, in fact, a recent study conducted by researchers at the Wharton School of Business has concluded that this activity — which they dubbed the wildcard option — does indeed take place, and can be quite profitable for those in the know.

According to the study, entitled, "The Wildcard Option in Transacting Mutual-Fund Shares" (Chalmers and Kadlec, 2000), individual investors who judiciously time their purchases and sales to take advantage of this "option" can earn an additional 0.15% *per day* compared to a simple buy and hold strategy. In fact, the researchers claim that a small number of fund investors are taking advantage of this imperfection as evidenced by individual fund-flow data.

So what is the practical lesson in all of this? Well, you can't squeeze orange juice out of a dry orange peel. Illiquid stocks that are placed inside liquid mutual funds will always create valuation problems. This is especially true if mutual funds must post absolute Net Asset Values — and are forced to create a two-way market at this price — as opposed to buy and sell prices, like any other traded security.

In the Internet age, we have all become accustomed to instantaneous prices for all our financial assets. But the plain fact is that not everything can be priced in continuous time. As Heisenberg's (financial) uncertainty principle teaches us, the mere act of measuring can, in fact, distort.

Fund Fees and Frivolous Fights

16

Never before has so much been said about so little a number.

I am talking, of course, about MERs on mutual funds and the recent battle among companies to reduce their management fees and fund expenses by a few trivial basis points, and then advertise it widely. In an earlier chapter we discussed MERs, in this chapter we'll look at them again and focus on what they buy you.

Indeed, just a few months ago a well-known player in the financial services industry announced that their MERs would be lowered to only 0.14% per year, in contrast to a similar competitor's product, which was charging 0.17% per annum.

Just to remind you, the gross return earned on the stocks and bonds held in the mutual fund are reduced by the MER to arrive at the net annual return. This is the number that is reported in the newspaper and your quarterly statement. Think of the MER as the markup from buying stocks retail instead of wholesale.

MERs are charged regardless of the performance of the fund. Hence, while you may be willing to pay the MER for a fund with superior performance, paying the manager to lose your money is often difficult medicine to swallow.

To put these numbers in perspective, an MER of 0.17% per annum is equivalent to a fee of $17 for every $10,000 invested. The competitor's offer of an MER of 0.14% is equivalent to a savings of $3 on a $10,000 portfolio. Essentially, you get the equivalent of a small cup of designer coffee in exchange for your hard-earned nest egg.

Note that MERs of 0.17% or 0.14% are incredibly low, considering that the average MER in Canada is about 2.16%, or 216 basis points. Investing in a mutual fund of only 0.14%, or 14 basis points, represents a savings of 202 basis points for an individual invested in the average Canadian mutual fund, or 2.02%. To put this figure in context, for a $100,000, this represents a savings of $2,020 per year!

As I explained in an earlier chapter, these small numbers can add up to quite a lot of money in the long run. But, once you get down to the teens and single digits, can an additional basis point make such a big difference?

Thus, I can understand switching from a mutual fund with a huge MER to a mutual fund with a tiny MER. But should we care about a few basis points? Does it make any sense to switch from one fund to another simply over a 0.03% difference in MER?

I'm not suggesting that you should ignore small differences in MERs. In fact, it's not difficult to demonstrate that small differences in MERs can lead to significant differences in returns after a number of years.

A fascinating and comprehensive study in the August 2000 issue of *The Journal of Finance* sheds light on this issue. In his report, University of Maryland professor Russ Wermers examined the historical returns of actively managed mutual funds over the last 20 years. Specifically, he compared only the performance of the stocks within the fund — as opposed to the entire fund — to the general market indices.

He concluded that *on average*, during the period 1975 to 1994, mutual funds held stocks that outperformed the market indices by approximately 1.3% per year. But, on average, the net return to unit holders of these funds lagged the same market indices by about 1%. Thus, the difference between the gross return of their superior stock picks and the net return of their actual fund was 2.3% per year. Of this 2.3%, the article argues that 0.7% is attributed to the cash and bond "drag" — which forces funds into holding non-stocks in order to maintain liquidity for redemptions and outflows — and the remaining 1.6% is attributed to expenses and transaction costs. These results are displayed in Figure 4.

So, the following picture emerges. Mutual fund managers *do* know how to pick good stocks relative to the markets against which they are compared and benchmarked, but the costs of running the fund consume most of these excess returns. They earn just enough to pay their management expense fees.

In the author's own words: "...evidence indicates that the average mutual fund holds stocks with

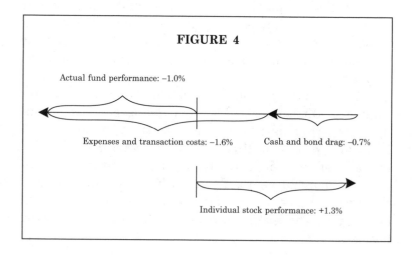

FIGURE 4

Actual fund performance: −1.0%

Expenses and transaction costs: −1.6%   Cash and bond drag: −0.7%

Individual stock performance: +1.3%

returns that compensate for the higher expenses and trading costs...."

Okay. So, knowing that fund mangers are earning their keep — but just barely — what are the practical and relevant lessons for the common investor?

Well, first of all, a lower MER on an actively managed mutual fund does not necessarily generate or preserve more wealth in the long run. It is counter-productive to chase low MERs just for their own sake. This is akin to shopping for a car by identifying those with the lowest markup instead of the highest quality. Indeed, it's quite likely that the higher markup — from wholesale to retail — may be worth the price.

However, if passively managed index funds (or exchange-traded participation units) are your cup of tea, then by all means seek out the ones with the lowest MERs, even though you may only be saving the equivalent of a cup of coffee per year.

As demonstrated above, while you receive superior performance from actively managed funds, you pay for it as well. A related question to explore is, do higher cost managers, in terms of MER, perform better? In other words, is there a positive relationship between MERs and performance? Or do all actively managed funds perform in a similar fashion?

This is an important question. If all actively managed funds perform in a similar fashion, then we indeed should be careful to observe whether the MER is 1.23 versus 1.10, for example. But if higher MERs suggest better performance, we must think twice before switching funds on the basis of MERs alone.

Another research study, published in the *Quarterly Review of Economics and Finance*, provides insight into this issue. The study relates MERs and performance, and shows that higher mutual fund expenses are associated with higher investment returns. Of course, this does not apply for every fund, and you may, indeed, be able to find a fund with both low MERs and superior performance. However, this study also suggests that changing funds on the basis of MERs alone is a mistake as well.

For example, consider a situation where you have $10,000 invested in mutual fund XYZ, which is expected to earn 15%, and has an MER equal to 2.50%. You are considering switching to another fund, mutual fund BCD, with a minuscule MER of 0.15%, which is expected to earn 11.5% in the coming year. Should you make the switch?

Well, your $10,000 in mutual fund XYZ will earn $1,500 for you after one year. But the MER over the period is $250. Hence, the net earnings are $1,250. If you switch your $10,000 to mutual fund BCD, the fund will earn $1,150 for you in one year. Subtracting the MER of $15, the net earnings are $1,135 — significantly less than the $1,250 earned on mutual fund XYZ.

As we see from the above example, we have to consider both expected return and MERs jointly to make investment allocation decisions that optimize our portfolios. Making decisions on the basis of MERs exclusively is irresponsible. Similarly, choosing investments on the basis of returns alone is irresponsible as well. As the earlier study demonstrates, there's no free lunch. While some investments may appear to provide superior performance, after considering the MERs, they may underperform passive index funds. In either event, for the small retail investor the battle of the MERs may be more marketing hype than a move towards efficient price competition.

So, How Much Do You Really Need at Retirement?

17

Ask two financial planners how much money you need to retire comfortably, and you will likely get three very different answers, but with similar invoices.

In the media, you often see numbers ranging from millions of dollars all the way down to nothing. Look closely, and you may notice that the recommended savings depends on the self-interest of the party making the recommendation. Companies that are in the business of selling savings vehicles have all the incentive to recommend that you save as much as possible. After all, they receive a percentage of your savings as management fees. Companies selling consumption and entertainment, such as the real estate industry or television manufacturers, might prefer that you spend your money today, and save as little as possible for retirement.

You face two risks when saving for retirement. On the one hand, you don't want to save "too little" money. What is too little? Well, if you outlive your money, or if you can't maintain the quality of life you are used to, then you have saved too little money. On the other hand, you don't want to save "too much" money. What is too much? Well, if you die with a huge nest egg, then maybe you've saved too much, as instead of saving your money, you could have consumed more during your lifetime. In other words, good news for your beneficiaries is bad news for you.

Now, I recognize that it's better to die with "too much" cash than with "too little". After all, you'll never know you died with too much cash, because you'll be, well, dead. On the other hand, you'll be very aware that you died with too little cash, because you may have to spend years struggling or depending on relatives, when you should be enjoying your retirement. However, if planning today can help you avoid dying with too much, you'll be able to increase your consumption during your entire retirement. And while money doesn't buy happiness, it can buy a few more days a month at the golf club. Hence, efficient retirement planning takes both the "too much" and "too little" risks into effect, though we'd rather lean towards "too much" rather than "too little".

So, how does a rational and prudent individual go about figuring the ideal nest egg, and how much they will need?

Personally, I believe the answer is that you should forget about size and simply take it only one year at a time. I call it the 35/65/95 rule. Here is how my strategy works. First, you don't even bother thinking about retirement planning until age 35. I am consistently baffled by the large number of people who are in their early twenties that are "worried" about the CPP and are saving for retirement — in 40 years. I say, deal with other worries first, such as developing a career and family.

Then, at age 36, worry about what you will need at age 66, which is exactly 30 years away. Then, at age 37 worry about 67, etc. Each and every year, you continue to think 30 years ahead. Finally, in the last year of saving, at age 65, you put some money aside for age 95, and immediately retire.

If you follow the 35/65/95 rule, you won't be overwhelmed with the task ahead. Instead of planning for your retirement, you plan for 30 separate single year retirements.

But how much must you save each year between 35 and 65 to fund your retirement?

Table 12 indicates how much of your current income you must save in order to have a certain standard of living in 30 years. I consider two standards of living. The first is the standard of living you can have with 75% of your current income. This is on the high side, as your expenses during retirement are likely to be lower. The second is the standard of living you can have with 60% of your current income, which is on the low side. In addition, I look at two possible investment portfolios. One that is tilted heavily towards equity-based products, and the other that consists primarily of fixed-income bonds. For each of the four scenarios I consider, I estimate the percentage of current income that must be saved in order to attain the specified standard of living, given the type of investment.

Critical to this entire analysis is my focus on the real (after-inflation) rate of return, as opposed to the nominal (pre-inflation) number. After all, to maintain

---

TABLE 12
The 35/65/95 Rule of Retirement Planning

Real Investment Return	Post-Retirement Standard of Living	
	75% of Current Income (high)	60% of Current Income (low)
7.5% (high, equity)	8.6%	6.8%
3.5% (low, bonds)	26.7%	21.4%

Note: Assumes historical investment returns. Going forward the expectation may differ.

Source: Author calculations.

a standard of living you must, at the very least, keep up with inflation.

For example, if you currently earn $100,000 per year and would like to have a $75,000 income in 30 years, you must save $8,600 if you are planning to invest most of it in the stock market, and $26,700 if the bulk goes to the bond market. Notice how important the investment allocation is in determining how much you have to save. Your willingness to take on the risks associated with equity greatly reduces the percentage of income you must put towards your retirement savings. Note that if you are generally pessimistic about equity markets, and think equities will have a tough time earning 7.5% real, then you must obviously save much more than 8.6% to get 75% of your current income.

Of course, the purists among you might worry: "What if I live beyond age 95? Isn't there a risk that I don't have enough if I only think 30 years ahead?" Indeed, a 65-year-old female has approximately a 20% chance of reaching age 95, and a male's chances are a little bit less than half of that. But in response, remember there is a strong chance that you won't make it to 95, leaving substantial leftovers. However, the danger associated with outliving your money is real, and you can find yourself at your most financially vulnerable when you are likely least able to change your financial situation, due to physical limitations associated with old age.

There are a number of ways to ensure you don't outlive your money. First, you can over-save for retirement. For example, you may wish to save assuming you will live to the age of 120. While I appreciate the optimism implicit with such a strategy, I question whether such a plan is realistic. After all, each year of additional retirement you save for costs you today — to the point where you limit consumption today in order to consume, with limited probability, at the age of 100. Such saving will likely overwhelm most income earners, particularly when there are more immediate bills to pay.

Second, you can try to make a deal with your children, as follows: If you exceed 95, they support you for the rest of your natural life. If you don't, they keep the difference. Many are reluctant to use such a strategy, due to the financial independence that must be sacrificed, albeit at an advanced age. Further, such agreement assumes that children will be able to support you at that age, which may not be the case. I can also imagine how such an arrangement can strain relationships, and may not be for everyone.

The third, and possibly the most advisable, method of ensuring you don't outlive your money is by both diversifying your investment and buying a life annuity, which I discuss in a later chapter.

To sum. First, forget about targeting a particular nest egg size, and focus on targeting consumption. Second, and more critically, *how* you save is much more important than *what* you save. It is meaningless to talk about saving rates without first worrying about what you plan to do with those savings. In the table, saving 25% (let alone 18%) of current income will *not* be enough, if you invest too conservatively.

Are Options an Option?

18

Listening to fund company executives, financial planners and the mainstream press, it seems that investments come in two basic colours: stocks and bonds. The former represents the equity of a company; the latter is the debt of a company, or perhaps of a government. Sure, there are different types of equity, like preferred and common; and debt can be callable, convertible or extendable. But these are just shades of the same general asset class. If the stock market takes a serious tumble — or for that matter, goes nowhere for the next 10 years — then regardless of what flavour of stocks you own, kiss the yacht goodbye. Likewise, if interest rates take off, your bond portfolio will suffer, no matter its exact composition.

Worse, investors whose portfolios are restricted to stocks and bonds have a narrow set of strategies to counter negative stock market or interest rate changes. They can sell their stocks or exchange cyclical stocks for defensive stocks if the stock market declines. They can exchange bonds for equity if they anticipate interest rates to rise. (Note: Cyclical stocks are stocks highly sensitive to changes in the GDP, such as stocks of companies that provide services to other companies. Defensive stocks, such as stocks of utility companies, are not very sensitive to changes in the GDP.)

These strategies provide limited flexibility. After all, it's quite likely that a crisis in one asset class — like an unexpected increase in interest rates — will strongly affect the other.

So, the issue I would like to address is: Is there anything else out there? Are there alternative asset classes, such as precious metals, agricultural commodities, foreign currencies, or even more exotic products like options and derivatives, that are worth buying in order to insulate and diversify your wealth from stocks and bonds? I believe the answer to this question is: Yes.

Indeed, I would argue that we might be doing our wealth a disservice by only focusing our attention on traditional and familiar investments. Personally, I think that 5% to 10% of one's investable wealth should be in non-traditional asset classes.

A recent study by two researchers at the University of Michigan, which was published in the *Journal of Finance* ("Expected Option Returns," June 2001), provides some evidence for the benefits of thinking outside the perennial box. According to Professors J. Coval and T. Shumway, selling options short — i.e., both calls and puts that you don't own — can be a profitable long-term investment strategy. They estimate an astonishing average return of 3% per week on S&P 500 options. The technical explanation for this quite large and puzzling return is that people who are willing to sell stock market insurance to others (short volatility, in the traders' lingo) are well compensated for the risk they are taking.

Okay. For those to whom this sounds like Greek, here is a quick refresher on options. A call option is a contract between two parties. It provides one party, designated the "long position", with the right, but not the obligation, to *buy* an underlying security at a fixed price (designated the exercise price) by a fixed date from the other party, designated the "short position". Note that while the long position has no obligation to buy the security, the short position is obligated to sell the security at the pre-specified price, should the long position wish to exercise his or her right.

For example, consider call options that trade on the XYZ Corporation. The current stock price for the XYZ Corporation is $102.50. Two individuals, Mr. Long and Ms. Short, sign a contract specifying the following agreement: Mr. Long, who has taken the long position, has the right to purchase from Ms. Short, who has taken the short position, a single share of XYZ Corporation in three months for $100. In return, Mr. Long agrees to pay $3 to Ms. Short immediately.

When will Mr. Long choose to exercise his right? Let's consider two scenarios.

In the first scenario, the price of XYZ Corporation stock has increased to $110. In this scenario, Mr. Long will exercise his right. After all, he can make riskless profit through simply exercising his right to buy the stock, and then selling the stock for the market price. His profit is equal to the selling price minus the purchase price, or $110 minus $100, resulting in a profit of $10. Of course, the cost of the option was $3, hence the net profit is less than $10.

In the second scenario, the price of XYZ Corporation stock has decreased to $90. In this scenario, Mr. Long will not exercise his right. After all, why purchase the stock for $100, as specified in the option contract, when he can easily purchase it for $90 on the market? In this scenario, Ms. Short is the one who profits, as she received $3 for taking the short position — but never had to sell the stock.

From this example, we see that a call option will only be exercised if the market price in three months is greater than the exercise price.

A put option is the exact opposite of a call option. It is the right, but not the obligation, to *sell* an underlying security at a fixed price by a fixed date. This is where it gets confusing: In a put option, the party with the right to sell is the long position. Contrast to a call option, where the party with the right to buy is the long position. To overcome the confusion, think of it this way: When it comes to options, whoever has the *right* is the *long* position. Whoever has the *obligation* is the *short* position. In a put option, while the long position has no obligation to sell the security, the short position is obligated to buy the security at the pre-specified price, should the long position wish to exercise his or her right.

Let's return to our previous example. Let's say Mr. Long and Ms. Short sign another contract. This contract specifies the following agreement: Mr. Long, who has taken the long position, has the right to sell a single share of XYZ Corporation to Ms. Short for $100. In return, Mr. Long agrees to pay $0.25 to Ms. Short immediately.

When will Mr. Long choose to exercise his right? Let's consider the two scenarios we looked at earlier.

In the first scenario, the price of XYZ Corporation stock has increased to $110. In this scenario, Mr. Long will not exercise his right. After all, he can sell the stock on the market for $110, hence why would he bother to sell it to Ms. Short for $100?

In the second scenario, the price of XYZ Corporation stock has decreased to $90. In this scenario, Mr. Long will exercise his right. Mr. Long can make riskless profit through simply buying the stock on the market, and then exercising his right to sell the stock. As was the case in the call options example, his profit is equal to the selling price minus the purchase price, or $100 minus $90, resulting in a profit of $10. Of course, the cost of the option was $0.25, hence the net profit is less than $10.

To sum, you can buy calls and puts, and pay an option premium, or you can sell calls and puts and receive an option premium.

Remember that you can sell options that you do not own by committing to pay any liability that arises from this position. Hence, you do not have to own the stock at the time you take a short position in an option.

Now, back to the above-mentioned study. The authors claim that selling call options together with put options at the exact same time, affectionately known as a straddle, generates very high investment returns. Here is how to think about this. In Figure 5, if you sell call and put options, both with a delivery price of $100, you gain an immediate option premium. You are now in the position of an insurance

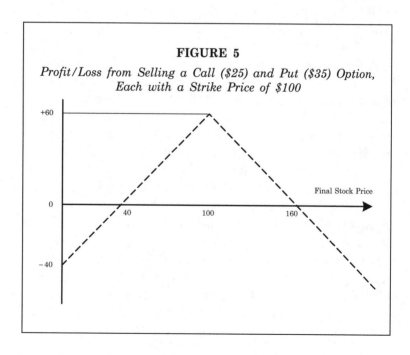

FIGURE 5

Profit/Loss from Selling a Call ($25) and Put ($35) Option, Each with a Strike Price of $100

company that is guaranteeing protection in exchange for premiums. As long as things don't go (too) wrong, you should make money from all the premiums you retained. In our case, if the underlying stock rises during the life of the option, up to $160 in the figure, the put option premium will exceed whatever you might have to pay out on the call option. Likewise, in the other direction. If the underlying stock falls during the life of the option, up to $40 in the diagram, the call premium will exceed whatever you might have to pay out on the put.

Now, although I certainly would not encourage my mother to start selling call and put options on her investment portfolio, this strategy seems to make sense for the more adventurous and knowledgeable investor. There is always the risk that the underlying stock will finish outside the $40 to $60 range, but you are well compensated for this risk, on average.

In any event, my main point is that you might want to consider some non-traditional investments for your nest egg, and the variety might do you good.

Owning a Piece of the Local Gas Station

19

Do you watch those numbers get higher and higher, and wonder why *your* investment portfolio can't increase at the same rate as the meter on the local gas pump? It now costs me $40 to top up my battered Topaz, and my hydro bill doesn't look any prettier. I'm not sure whether the large oil companies or the local merchants are making big bucks from the recent run-up, but I certainly would like to have a piece of that action.

Well, the truth is you can, with something called Energy Income Trusts — a type of investment within the income trusts family.

What is Energy Income Trusts? To the novice, it might sound like some offshore legal structure for the oil rich and famous, but in fact it is quite simple. They are just as easy to understand and use as Mutual Fund Trusts or Real Estate Trusts. And most of them trade like stocks on the Toronto Stock Exchange.

Technically speaking, an Energy Income Trust (sometimes known as an Oil and Gas Royalty Trust) is created in order to acquire, develop and produce crude oil and natural gas properties. The idea is to manage a collection of these properties in an effective and efficient manner so it can provide you with income on a regular basis and in a tax efficient manner. The owner of the units (read: you) is then entitled to a stream of royalty income from a variety of natural resource properties.

The managers of the trusts sell these units to the public and then use the money to finance more exploration and development projects, which then yield more royalty income, etc. The managers distribute a large percentage of the cash generated from the company's assets to the unit holders on a monthly basis. But they do keep some for reinvestment.

To illustrate, let's use an example. Consider the ARC Energy Income Trust, which is (not surprisingly) situated in Calgary, in the oil-rich province of Alberta, and trades on the TSE. According to the trust managers, ARC Energy Income Trust has completed over $1.4 billion worth of asset acquisitions since its inception in 1996. As the oil and natural gas earn revenues, ARC receives a 99% royalty, which is then paid to unit holders as cash distribution. However, before distribution, deductions are first made for various charges, such as capital expenditures.

One interesting feature of Energy Income Trust is that they hold a collection of properties, not just a single one; hence, they take advantage of the diversification effect. Indeed, two types of risks are diversified: the risks associated with the properties, and the risks associated with the exploration that takes place on the properties. However, because of its focus on the energy industry, risks that are industry wide are not reduced.

For example, a position in (owning) an Energy Income Trust Unit will reduce the risk associated with exploration failure at a single property (such as the recent abandonment of an offshore exploratory well near Nova Scotia by ChevronTexaco Corp.), or an accounting scandal perpetrated by the managers of one company (the infamous Enron scandal). But if peace or war breaks out in the Middle East, the

entire Energy Income Trust Unit will be affected —
for better or worse.

Now, given the regular source of income payments these units produce, some investors might con-
fuse them with fixed-income bonds or debentures.
Careful, these units are certainly not anything near
as safe or as reliable as a bond mutual fund. If the
underlying assets (read: oil and gas wells) depreciate,
you may see a declining price for the units on the
stock exchange.

In their defence, however, many of them do generate income that is higher than the interest rates
on long-term bonds. This is because of the risk–
return tradeoff, a fundamental rule of modern finance
theory: If you accept high risk, you are compensated
with higher expected return. The greater income associated with Energy Income Trusts may be due to the
higher risk associated with them than with a bond
fund.

So far, we've demonstrated the diversification and
income characteristics of Energy Income Trusts: two
features that would make them attractive investment
choices for those who wish to have exposure to energy
market movements. But an even better feature of
Energy Income Trusts is that a portion of this income
is tax advantaged. For tax purposes, they are considered to be flow-through vehicles that allow individual investors to claim tax-shelter deductions with
a liability limit to the amount they invested. Many
companies structure their trust units to maximize
the portion of total distribution as a return of capital.
This allows the holder to defer paying income taxes,
for a while at least.

An alternative investment through which investors can gain exposure to changes in energy prices —
whether for hedging and diversification purposes, or
as speculation — is derivative securities.

How can derivative securities be used for hedging purposes? There are many ways, as discussed in energy industry journals. The use of more complex derivative securities — such as swaps and collars — to hedge energy prices is beyond the scope of this chapter. Instead, I will explain it through the use of a simple derivative security, the futures contract.

So, what is a futures contract? As mentioned in an earlier chapter, a futures contract is similar to a call option, except neither the buy nor the sell party has any rights; both are obligated to transact at the specified date, regardless of market price. To illustrate, consider a futures contract involving the sale of 300 barrels of oil between Mr. X and Ms. Y. Mr. X is obligated to purchase 300 barrels of oil from Ms. Y, at a price of $33 per barrel of oil, three months in the future. If actual market oil price in three months goes up, let's say, to $36, then Mr. X profits and Ms. Y loses. After all, Mr. X can purchase the barrels of oil for $33, then turn around and sell them on the market for $36, pocketing a profit of ($3 × 300 =) $900. But should actual market oil price drop to $22, then Ms. Y profits, and Mr. X loses. Bound by the contract, Mr. X must purchase the barrels of oil at $33, while Ms. Y can ensure a supply of the barrels for the market price of $22, resulting in a profit of ($11 × 300 =) $3,300.

Now, let's use the same information with the aid of Figure 6 to present the power of hedging using basic futures contracts.

Consider Ms. Y as the head of an energy firm that holds many barrels of oil. Ms. Y is afraid that energy prices will go down, thereby destroying firm value. To hedge this risk, she uses short futures contracts. Let's turn to the figure now.

In the figure, Ms. Y's goal is represented by the broken line — the total portfolio value, which remains at $33 regardless of the rise and fall of oil value. The

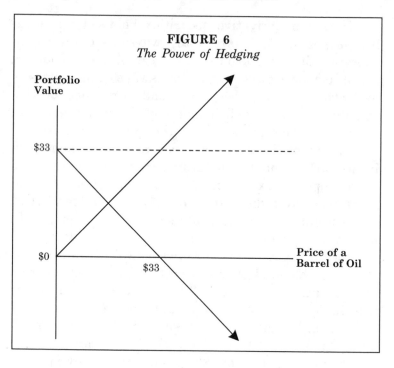

FIGURE 6
The Power of Hedging

upward sloping line represents the payoff from a single position in a barrel of oil. The higher the price of oil, the higher the portfolio value. The downward sloping line represents a single short futures contract, with a $33 pre-specified price. If the market price is also $33, then the value of the position is zero. If value is above $33, then the value of the futures contract is negative, but it is positive if the value is below $33. Here's how hedging with futures contracts works. When the value of a barrel of oil goes up to $42, the position in a single barrel of oil is $42, and the value of the short futures contract is negative $9. Conversely, when the value of a barrel of oil goes down to $24, the position in a single barrel of oil would be $24, and the value of the short futures contract would be positive $9. The net result, in both situations (price increase and decrease), is a portfolio value of $33. The same applies for every possible price of a barrel of oil.

Note that individual investors may have a difficult time hedging through the use of derivative securities. First, there are transaction costs, which may be too costly for an individual. Second, there are dangers associated with the use of derivative securities — ask Orange County — and many individual investors may not have the confidence required. Hence the role of Energy Income Trusts: To provide individual investors with the ability to hedge or speculate on energy prices without overburdensome expenses or consumption of time.

So, where does this fit in terms of your overall portfolio? Should you sell the house and the blue-chip stock and load up on Energy?

Well, let's not go too far in diversifying our assets. One of the benefits of holding some of these trusts, as I alluded to earlier, is that you can use them to *hedge* your fuel and energy costs. Think of it as insurance against $50 for a barrel of crude oil. Large corporations can purchase insurance against rising fuel costs (they use derivatives), but it's tough for you and me to get this type of policy. But, you can create the same effect on a smaller scale with investments that shine in rising fuel costs environments. Of course, if the price of gas drops substantially, there is a chance your Energy Income Trusts will take a hit, but then again, your day-to-day living expenses should drop as well. If only we could do this for kids' braces!

Stocks: In or Out (of the RRSP)?

20

By now, you must have all heard about the term "asset allocation". It refers to the critical importance of diversifying, or spreading your wealth across different asset classes or mutual fund categories. But recently, a new term has been gaining currency in the investment vocabulary. It is called asset "location" (as opposed to allocation). Apparently, where you put your assets is just as important as which assets you choose to own.

I am talking, of course, about whether your investments, such as mutual funds, stocks and bonds, should be located *inside* tax-sheltered trusts like Registered Retirement Savings Plans (RRSP), or whether they should be placed *outside* the shelter.

The rationale behind asset location is completely different than the rationale behind asset allocation, but both are extremely important considerations. The objective of asset *allocation* is to lower diversifiable risk, thereby reducing risk without changing expected returns. The objective of asset *location* is to make sure your investments are strategically located so as to legally minimize taxes.

In this chapter, I will examine the following question: If you are saving more than your RRSP limit, and if stocks are to be part of your portfolio, where should they be located?

There are benefits associated with RRSPs that are unquestionable. One we all immediately think of is the tax savings associated with RRSPs. But in my opinion, there is a benefit more important than the tax implications. Namely, the perception of tax sheltering associated with RRSPs that motivates individuals to save — saving that they would likely not do otherwise.

Consider a typical hard working father, trying to support his three children and his wife, who is a stay-at-home mom. Even with a modest home and car, after the government takes its huge bite out of his earnings, the last thing he would think about is retirement — there are much more pressing needs today, such as paying the cell phone bill and the mortgage. It's not that retirement is ignored, but how can the father think 30 or 40 years ahead, when he has such pressing financial demands today? Without the motivation provided by the tax deferral associated with an RRSP, little to no retirement saving would take place.

Indeed, this motivation is the reason why the federal government permitted tax sheltering in an RRSP in the first place. Of course, in a perfect world, individuals would recognize the need to save for retirement, and make sure to do so, regardless of external motivations. In reality, however, we have difficulty thinking so far ahead, especially when we may be struggling monthly to make the car and mortgage payments.

Now, let's return to the question of asset location. Imagine that you own some solid blue-chip stock mutual funds and some diversified bond funds. Should you place the bonds inside an RRSP, or outside?

Conventional wisdom argues as follows. The investment return from stocks, which is comprised of dividend income and capital gains, is taxed more lightly than interest income from bonds. Thus, you don't need a tax shelter for the stocks, and should, therefore, only use the RRSP for the bonds. At first glance, this makes a lot of sense, and is practised widely; bonds inside, stocks outside.

But, in fact, some new "probabilistic" thinking, backed by empirical research in the United States, suggests that the above-mentioned rule of thumb may not be correct in all cases. And, in fact, there is an argument to be made for placing bonds outside, despite the higher taxes they attract, and stocks inside.

But, before I discuss the avant-garde thinking, let's go back to basics and review the advantages associated with RRSPs to begin with.

There are three reasons why you might want to use a Registered Retirement Savings Plan. But there are also three reasons why you might want to avoid RRSPs. Normally, the former reasons outweigh the drawbacks of the latter, and the RRSP is a good deal. But occasionally, you are better off avoiding RRSP investments.

Let's review the three reasons why RRSPs are beneficial. First, you get to defer taxes on both the original income as well as any gains, until you withdraw the funds. And you'd much rather pay your tax bill in 10 to 20 years than today.

Second, you might be in a lower tax bracket at that time, which means that you pay even less. For example, you might be in the 45% tax bracket prior to retirement, but only in the 30% bracket during your golden years. So you would rather pay tax (later) at a rate of 30%, compared to now, at a rate of 45%

Third, as mentioned earlier, RRSPs are beneficial as they motivate individuals to save who may otherwise not be inclined to do so.

On the opposite side, the three reasons you might want to avoid using an RRSP are the way that Canada Customs and Revenue Agency recognizes withdrawn cash, the illiquidity associated with RRSPs, and the foreign restriction associated with RRSPs. Let's consider each in turn.

The first disadvantage associated with RRSPs is that all gains — when you withdraw money — will be considered ordinary interest, regardless of source. So, for example, if your RRSP earned $50,000 in capital gains, you have to pay tax at the Ordinary Income Rate, which could be as high as 50% or higher, instead of the much lower capital gains rate.

The second disadvantage associated with RRSPs is that they generate inherent illiquidity should you have the need to withdraw the cash before retirement. For example, consider a situation where an individual faces a family emergency that results in a $50,000 expenditure. At the 50% tax bracket, the individual will have to withdraw $100,000 from his RRSP — $50,000 to cover the tax associated with withdrawing funds from the RRSP, and $50,000 to cover the family expense. There are mechanisms, such as spousal RRSPs and first time home buyers plans, that mitigate the tax penalty associated with withdrawing funds from an RRSP, but these mechanisms are not available or appropriate in many situations.

The third disadvantage is the foreign content restrictions associated with RRSPs. The government mandated these restrictions to support capital markets in Canada. But the restrictions also limit the diversification capabilities of individual investors. Fortunately, as mentioned in an earlier chapter, the investment industry has found a way to overcome foreign content restrictions through the use of "clone funds".

The above advantages and disadvantages are well known, and the persistent popularity of RRSPs indicates that, for most investors, the advantages outweigh the disadvantages. Conventional wisdom is clear: It's better to invest cash inside an RRSP than outside. And, I completely agree with that. In other words, if you have the room, use it, unless you are in a very low tax (and income) bracket and might have better use for the room in future years.

However, the issue I'm addressing here is the question of location. Imagine that you have $500 worth of stocks, and $500 worth of bonds, but only $500 of RRSP room in your tax shelter. Remember that, regardless of whether you place the stocks and bonds inside or outside, you will get a tax deduction for the contribution, and a subsequent refund from the tax authorities. The main issue at hand is that some of your investments will have to remain unsheltered, and the question is which. As I mentioned earlier, the conventional wisdom would be to place the $500 worth of bonds inside, and the $500 worth of stocks outside.

But, according to Professors J. Poterba and J. Shoven, both researchers at Stanford University and the National Bureau of Economic Research (Working paper #7991), putting the highly taxed assets (i.e., bonds) *inside* a tax shelter and lightly taxed assets (i.e., stocks) *outside* a tax shelter might be doing your wealth a disservice in the long run. Although their study is focused on the U.S. retirement savings market, I believe the same could hold true in Canada as well.

While the actual results would depend on the return from the stocks, here is an artificial case that illustrates the main point.

Figure 7 displays the benefit (and loss) from adopting the conventional wisdom.

As you can see from the figure, if you are planning on maintaining the RRSP for less than 20 years, then you are indeed better off using the conventional wisdom and placing the stocks outside the tax sheltered RRSP. In fact, the relative value of the conventional wisdom is quite large. For example, after 15

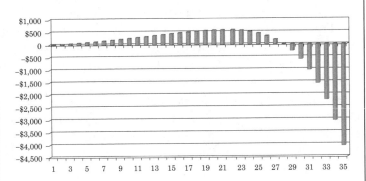

FIGURE 7

Benefit (and Loss) of Holding Stocks Outside RRSP

Ordinary Income Tax Rate: 50%
Capital Gains Tax Rate: 25%
Investment Return: 9% Realized Capital Gains + 6%
Unrealized Capital Gains = 15% per annum

Note: Though the 15% p.a. gains may appear high, the point of
this example is to illustrate the stocks may belong inside an
RRSP in some situations.

Source: Author calculations.

years — by properly placing the stocks outside — you
would be ahead by $650 on an after-tax basis. The
reason for this follows from the earlier logic. The
interest income attracts higher taxes, which is why
you are ahead by keeping it sheltered and the stocks
outside.

But — and here is my main argument — as your
savings horizon gets longer, the value of the conventional wisdom becomes negative. With a 30-year
savings horizon, you are better off placing the stocks
inside the RRSP, and the bonds *outside* the RRSP.

You actually lose $3,600 — relatively speaking — if you follow the conventional wisdom.

This (non-linear) result should seem quite odd at first, and it certainly requires explanation.

The intuition for this result is as follows. Up to now, we have ignored the question of returns, and focused exclusively on taxes. And, in fact, if stocks and bonds were to earn the exact same pre-tax investment return, then conventional wisdom would be 100% correct, and stocks would always be placed outside the shelter. Indeed, with equal pre-tax return, the graph would always result in positive numbers, regardless of the time horizon.

But stocks tend to earn more than bonds, and with increasing certainty as the horizon increases. Moreover, equity mutual funds don't do a particularly good job of reducing turnover. Thus, although capital gains are taxed more lightly — and only when the gains are realized — mutual funds as a whole don't seem to take advantage of this fact. In other words, you tend to pay more (and sooner) tax than you think when holding equities outside the shelter.

Think of it this way. In the above example, your $500 of stocks is likely to grow to $5,000 by the time you retire, but you will be lucky if the $500 of bonds grows to $1,000 over the same period. So, if the (enormous) capital gains on the stock portfolio are only realized at retirement, then, sure, go ahead and keep them outside the shelter. But, if these very large stock investment gains will accrue and be realized along the way, you might be better off placing the stocks inside the tax shelter — even if this means you will have to pay large ordinary income taxes on gains when you pull the money out. In this particular case, taking all the pain at the end may be more effective than a little bit of pain each year along the way.

Now, granted, the picture I have shown you is very much dependent on the underlying assumptions and implicit realization rates. For other parameters and situations, the outcome and conclusions might be reversed. But, at the very least, this line of thinking should make you pause and think about what goes where.

Also, a further reason for keeping the stock mutual funds inside the RRSP, and the bond funds outside, is pure liquidity. In case of an emergency you should tap your non-RRSP money before raiding the RRSP. And, if the stock funds are outside, you might be forced to sell at an inopportune (a.k.a. bear market) time. Finally, some innovative mutual fund companies have recently managed to design funds similar to money market and bonds funds that attract partial capital gains treatment by using options and futures to recycle interest into capital.

Of course, as the capital gains inclusion rate gets reduced further in Canada — currently it is down to 50% — the novel argument for putting stocks inside an RRSP will diminish. Furthermore, if the capital gains inclusion rate ever goes to zero, or for that matter, with zero turnover fund units (stocks that are never sold inside the fund; a true buy-and-hold strategy) I would keep all my stock funds outside, and bond funds inside. While we wait for Ottawa to lower the tax rate, the objective is not to minimize taxes, but to maximize your after-tax rate of return. The key message to remember is that location is just as important as allocation.

Mortgages: Fixed or Floating?

21

Despite my long-term pessimism about real estate as an investment, my wife finally convinced me that it is time to buy a house, since our small apartment can no longer accommodate our growing family. To make things easier, we have agreed that she will locate the house, while I arrange the financing. At first, I thought my job was the easier one, but with the numerous mortgage choices like open versus closed, fixed versus floating and capped versus floored, I'm starting to regret the division of labour.

So how does a rational consumer make sense of the bewildering array of products and strategies?

Well, the most important decision appears to be between fixed and floating mortgage arrangements. With a fixed-rate mortgage, your monthly payments are pre-determined and known in advance, throughout the entire term of the mortgage. The most common term is five years at a time. In contrast, with a floating rate mortgage, your payments will change from month to month depending on the value of the floating rate at the time of payment. In general, the floating rate tends to be linked to the prime business rate, although some arrangements might contain "caps" on how high the rates can go, and perhaps even "floors" on how low they can drop. For example, as I'm writing this, floating rate mortgages are at

4.25%, while five-year fixed-rate mortgages are close to 7.00%.

Now, the first thing to note is that interest rate movements are notoriously difficult to predict in advance, so trying to pick your mortgage term based on where you think rates are going can be a costly mistake.

So, in order to find the best value for my money in the long run, I did some statistical research to determine which strategy would have worked best in the past. I'll describe the research below. But before I do so, note that I am not the first, and definitely will not be the last, to examine the issue of optimal mortgage financing. The business press is replete with financial commentary and advice on the best ways to choose mortgage rates. Many popular personal finance books on buying homes contain similar nuggets of wisdom on mortgage financing. Indeed, many public commentators have argued that borrowing at short (floating) rates is preferable to locking in at longer (fixed) rates; my own data certainly provides support for their argument.

Unfortunately, most of the existing folklore and advice are rarely subjected to formal statistical analysis and do not address the probability that a given strategy will be successful. After all, the future is random, and there is always a chance that the current situation may change drastically. It is therefore inappropriate to say that one strategy is invariably better than the other, without quantifying the risks and benefits.

In reviewing the research — mostly based on the U.S. market — I find strong support for the notion that borrowing at a short-term floating rate will result in lower financing costs. Obviously, there are difficulties inherent in extrapolating from these results so that they are comparable to the Canadian environment. The U.S. mortgage and interest-rate environment is structurally unique because of the prevalence of longer-term mortgages (up to 25 years), the deductibility of mortgage interest payments from income taxes, and the increased flexibility to prepay (or even the ease to default) on a residential mortgage.

Consumers, for the most part, are not able to evaluate and compute the present value of their mortgage decisions. As a result, they cannot determine how costly their decisions might be in the long run, and which decision is superior on a present-value basis. In other words, consumers have a hard time quantifying the consequences of paying half a percent more, or less, on a mortgage over long periods of time.

But that's exactly what I did in my research — quantify the consequences of decisions, so that the dimension of your financial risk is clearer.

We already know that consumers make very different payments during the life of a mortgage, depending on whether they borrow long or short. Those who go short will have to renew their mortgage more frequently, and for differing periods and amounts. Those who borrow long will be able to fix their financing costs for longer periods of time, but at the expense of a reduction in flexibility. The question is: How do we compare the costs and benefits from using one financing strategy as opposed to the other?

I imagined two different people, Ms. Linda Long and Ms. Shelly Short. By chance, both of them are about to renew their mortgage, of which the current outstanding value is exactly $100,000. They intend to amortize their mortgage (i.e., completely pay off the loan after) over 15 years. Linda Long has decided to refinance her mortgage at the five-year fixed rate, while Shelly Short has decided to go floating by borrowing at the prime business rate.

So which consumer has made the smarter decision — Shelly or Linda?

Let us compare the total amount of interest paid
by both Shelly and Linda. The way to do this is as
follows. For each of the 180 monthly mortgage payments (over 15 years), I subtracted Shelly's payment
from Linda's payment to get the monthly savings
from going short versus long. This number may, in
fact, be negative if floating rates were higher than
fixed rates at that particular time. I then took the
monthly savings and computed the future value of the
funds at the time the mortgage was completely paid
off. By future value, I mean that I factored in any
interest income that Shelly (or Linda) might earn on
the savings.

For example, if Shelly paid $750 on her mort-
gage, while Linda paid $800 during the same month,
the savings from going short versus long would be
$50, which we then grow at the appropriate rate, to
obtain the value of savings at maturity. After all, one
dollar today is worth much more than one dollar in
15 years. I am just as concerned about *when* Linda
and Shelly have paid the interest as about *how
much* interest they have paid. So this adjustment is
important.

The important part is that I ran this analysis
for each month for each of the last 50 years. Specifically, I computed how much money Shelly would
save (or lose) from having her payments fluctuate
each and every month. Following this approach, I
was amazed to discover average maturity savings of
$22,210 for Shelly. In fact, in 85% of the cases Shelly
saved at least $10,000 by borrowing short (prime)
versus five-year fixed. Remember that this is on a
$100,000 mortgage, so the gains can be substantial.

Now, this result should not be too surprising. As
you can see from Figure 8, floating (prime) rates are
usually lower than five-year fixed mortgage rates.

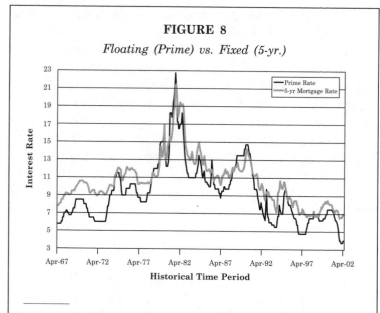

FIGURE 8

Floating (Prime) vs. Fixed (5-yr.)

Source: M.A. Milevsky, "Mortgage Financing: Floating Your Way to Prosperity," The IFID Centre Research Paper #01-01. Available on-line at <www.the-ifid-centre.ca>.

During the last 30 years, this was the norm 85% of the time. And the few periods during which floating rates were higher didn't last very long.

Until now, I have illustrated the savings that derive from borrowing short versus long without explaining why there should be a saving in the first place. Now, let me address the question of why this works out to be the case.

The main reason offered by economists is that short-term interest rates (like prime) are actually supposed to be lower than long-term interest rates (such as five-year mortgage rates). The higher long-term rates are to compensate banks, trust companies and other lenders for the greater uncertainty they face by lending longer. Clearly, they are tying up their money for a longer period of time. The longer the period, the greater the chance that interest rates will go up. If this occurs, financial institutions could lend out funds at the higher interest rate — if the funds were not already committed. On funds already lent out, any change in interest rates will have a bigger impact on the value of their asset (a mortgage or other loan). Indeed, the longer the time until the loan matures, the greater the impact. To compensate for this risk, they charge more. Thus, as I suggested earlier, when you borrow money for longer periods of time (read: at a fixed rate), you are paying a price for the stability. The price goes directly to the financial institution making the loan, to compensate and pay them for the instability they face.

For example, a 1% (or 100 basis point) increase in interest rates will have a significantly larger impact on a bank's long-term assets, like bonds, mortgages and other loans (depending on their exact maturity), than on its short-term assets. This is because the effect of the interest hike is felt for so much longer. Indeed, the value of the long-term assets will decline much more than that of the short-term assets.

This phenomenon is a reflection of the financial fact that asset prices are inversely related to interest rates. When interest rates rise, fixed-yield assets decline in value and short-term assets rise. Let's suppose that, due to interest-rate hikes, lenders are able to obtain assets that generate higher yields than those issued earlier. To be competitive with these new financial instruments, older ones must have the same effective yield as the new ones. To do so, they must fall in price.

Let's illustrate the principle with a bond that does not mature. You'll have to trust me that although this simplifies the analysis, it does not change the basic principle. Suppose that this perpetual bond is issued at $1,000 and pays $50 per annum in interest for a yield of 5%. Suddenly, interest rates rise to 10%, so that a newly issued bond without a maturity date pays $100 per annum in interest — for a yield of 10%. Now, the first bond issued must fall in price to $500 in order to yield 10%. Bonds that mature will not have to fall that far because, at maturity, the bond will be redeemed for $1,000, which compensates for some of the payoff difference and, hence, helps increase the yield to 10%. However, the longer the time to maturity, the more their price will have to decline. A bond with a 30-year maturity will have to decline almost that far in price, whereas one that matures in a year only has to fall a little in price.

Now, in spite of the general tendency for short-term interest rates to be lower than long-term rates, there are occasions when the yield curve becomes inverted. In other words, long-term rates become lower than short-term rates. By inverted — in the context of mortgages — we mean that five-year rates are lower than prime. In the common usage of the term, it represents cases in which yields (interest rates) on long-term government bonds are lower than those on short-term T-Bills. If and when this happens, it's quite likely that long-term mortgage rates will be lower than short-term (floating) rates, and the previously mentioned spread will be negative. But this phenomenon is rare.

In general, yield-curve inversions are indicative of a situation in which the central bank is implementing extremely tight monetary policy in order to fight actual or potential inflation. The central bank — by removing funds from the chartered banks to reduce their lending capabilities or by selling bonds to the public in exchange for money — can actually decrease the money supply or just slow down its rate of growth. This money squeeze or credit restriction has the effect of raising interest rates. It's simply a demand and supply situation: When there is relatively less money around, demand for what is available rises. However, these monetary instruments tend to work chiefly on short-term funds, leaving long-term rates relatively less affected. Thus, the so-called credit crunch is seen more at the short end of the yield curve than at the long end.

In the 50-year period considered in my analysis, there have only been two major inversions of the yield curve in the five-year range. These occurred between 1979 and 1982, the time of the second "oil shock" that came in response to the Iranian Revolution; and again, between 1989 and 1991, when Bank of Canada governor John Crow instituted a "zero inflation" policy that required an extremely tight monetary policy. In both of these instances, the rate inversion was quite severe.

In the past decade both the Canadian and U.S. economies experienced an extremely long expansion phase. In other words, economic growth continued unabated without a downturn in output. Central banks did not have to step in and apply the brakes in order to curtail excessive inflation by raising nominal interest rates significantly. Consequently, there was no tendency for long-term rates (five years, in our example) to be lower than short-term rates.

Over the last couple of years, central bankers have lowered rates to stimulate economic activity. Given the continuing rapid pace of technological change, the slowing rates of growth in North American economies and increased globalization, there seems even less likelihood that Shelly Short will pay more on her mortgage than Linda Long. In fact, for the foreseeable future, the norm is likely to be lower short-term interest rates compared to long-term rates. Which in turn means Shelly Short will continue to have the winning strategy.

Here are some further issues you might want to consider when taking out a mortgage.

1. For consumers who are refinancing their mortgages, as opposed to first-time homebuyers, I would recommend floating-rate loans. Because they are more experienced in mortgage matters and have some equity in their home, they can tolerate fluctuations in payments more.

2. The cyclical nature of economies and interest rates dictates that when rates are high, compared to historical averages, they tend to move back down. Likewise, when rates are low, they tend to move back up. Unfortunately, looking forward, it is extremely difficult to predict exactly when a cycle will end, and how low (or high) rates will still go. Therefore, I advise consumers to refrain from speculating on the future direction of interest rates, and instead, focus on their budgeting ability to withstand fluctuating mortgage payments.

3. Financing a mortgage at the short (floating) rate typically endows the consumer with an option to lock in future financing if they so desire. The reverse is not true. Consumers that borrow long, but decide to terminate (break) their mortgage in order to refinance at lower costs, usually face three to four months of interest penalty. The lack of symmetry provides another reason for going short, not long.

4. The long-term mortgage rates posted by banks and other financial institutions are always negotiable. In some cases, you might end up paying 1.5% (150 basis points) less than the advertised number. This negotiability is a recent trend in

mortgage financing, which casts doubt on the relevance of documented mortgage rates during the last decade. It's important for two reasons. First, you have more bargaining power than you think. And second, the savings to be derived from going short versus long might not be as high (nor as volatile) as they were in the past.

In sum, if your financial budget can handle fluctuation in payments, it appears that hitching your mortgage to a floating (prime) interest rate will result in the lowest interest costs. Long-term stability is costly when it comes to your mortgage payments.

Again, if you go short, you're taking some risk — the risk that at the end of your term, mortgage rates will have risen. If that's a risk you can't tolerate, financially or psychologically, then by all means go long (a.k.a. fixed). But generally, you are more likely to save money by taking the risk.

Do Eggs Belong in Baskets?

22

The famous economist John Maynard Keynes was once quoted as saying that he did not believe in diversifying his investments — he felt that you should simply buy a few good stock investments, and hold on to them.

Of course, the key word here is "good". It's always easy to identify good investments after the fact. And there is some evidence that Keynes was good at speculating before the fact as well: While in Cambridge University in the 1920s, Keynes made a fortune speculating in currency markets. This was between his work as a civil servant and his marriage to a Russian ballerina — I recommend you read one of the numerous biographies of Keynes if you'd like to fill in the gaps in his life story.

But Keynes' early success at speculation doesn't mean we will all do equally well. In fact, modern finance theory argues that it's impossible to identify good investments before the fact, unless you (illegally) use insider information.

Let me be perfectly clear: I don't mean that it's impossible to identify good companies before investing. Indeed, it's quite simple. Financial analysts have numerous ways of evaluating whether a company is good or not — such as revenue, earnings, management reputation and other measures. But a good *company* is not the same as a good *investment*. Modern finance theory argues that markets are efficient: they immediately update stock prices based on all publicly available information. Therefore, the fact that the company is "good" is already built into the stock price.

So, while it is possible to identify a good company, there is no guarantee that investing in the company is a good idea. Hence, buying a few good stocks, as Keynes recommends, is much easier said than done. Indeed, if Keynes were alive today, I wonder if he would have been a Nortel, or high-tech, casualty. Surely, buying a few good stocks doesn't work as well as it used to (if it ever did), and it's pretty much accepted wisdom that diversifying your investments makes good business sense.

"Don't put all your eggs in one basket" was a philosophy preached long before the emergence of modern portfolio theory. The world has recognized the need to diversify one's portfolio for at least two millennia. In fact, the Babylonian Talmud, compiled more than 2,000 years ago, recommends that a person split his or her wealth into three parts. One-third should be placed in real estate, one-third in money, and the remaining third in business assets, which I liberally interpret to include equities. Overall, not bad investment advice, especially if you could have followed it for the last 2,000 years.

But in all seriousness, why does diversification work? And why is it so important? After all, there is nothing inherently magical about splitting your money into many small parts and putting each part into a different investment vehicle. The benefit does not derive from the process of splitting the money, or placing it into different stocks.

For example, consider two companies. Both companies produce toothbrushes, and nothing else. Both compete in the same markets, and are approximately the same size. There will be differences in the stock performance of the two firms: one may have better management, or sign better contracts, or build a better toothbrush. Or, one firm may simply be luckier than the other. But stock performance is not related to firm-specific performance or luck exclusively. Instead, stock performance is related to many factors, including industry-specific factors and macroeconomic factors.

Now, consider an investor who splits his or her funds between these two companies. The investor gains some protection against firm-specific events, such as poor management of one of the companies. However, should the industry fail, or the macroeconomy falter, the investor will face financial disaster.

Thus, diversification is about more than simply placing money into different stocks. Rather, it's the relative movement of these investments that's important. In other words, how do they behave, move and grow over time? Do they move in lockstep? If one zigs, does the other zag? Obviously, this is a critically important question, because if the various investments all move in the same direction at the same time, up or down, you're not likely to benefit very much from diversifying. If they're all moving up, you might as well pick one fund, or stock for that matter, and stick with it. And if they're all moving down, then again, diversification clearly hasn't helped.

Indeed, the key — and the secret — to successful diversification is an old axiom: opposites attract. In investment terms, that means you want to diversify into sectors of the global and local economies that do not share the same up and down influences. For example, if you invest in both the financial services sector and the consumer products sector, you hope that when one is faltering, the other is not. Or if you further diversify into oil and gas and other resource industries, then ideally, if the first two sectors suffer, the third will prosper. No matter how great, or large, a company is, remember that it is still only one company.

But is diversification really useful? After all, we've all read about the risk–return tradeoff associated with investing — the more risks you take on, the greater your return. Hence, why diversify, when diversification lowers risk? Doesn't this simply lower return as well?

The thundering answer from modern finance theory is, "No!" The reason diversification is so important is because it allows investors to reduce risk, without decreasing expected returns. Remember, there are two types of risks: non-diversifiable and diversifiable risks. The risk–return tradeoff applies only to non-diversifiable risks, but not to diversifiable risks. The reason is because although diversifiable risks can be easily eliminated through diversification, taking on these risks is not compensated with higher expected returns.

Diversification is, therefore, quite a powerful risk-reduction tool, which no investors can afford to bypass. If the investor's objective is to lower risk, diversification can lower risk while maintaining the same level of expected return as before. If the investor's objective is to increase expected return on investment, diversification can permit the investor to do so and still maintain the same level of risk.

While diversification is a good idea in theory, in practice, what is considered a "diversified portfolio"? Is a portfolio consisting of two stocks considered diversified? Three stocks? Or does a portfolio require hundreds, or thousands, of stocks to be considered diversified?

Over the years, many scholars and market observers have devised ways of quantifying the benefits from diversification. Although no general consensus has emerged for computing exactly how many stocks one should own in order to be properly diversi-

TABLE 13	
Number of Stocks (Randomly Selected) New York Stock Exchange	Risk Reduction
1	0%
2	42%
4	64%
6	70%
10	76%
20	81%
50	83%

Source: E. Elton and M. Gruber, *Modern Portfolio Theory* (New York: John Wiley, 1995).

fied, the main message is that it should be at least 10, and perhaps even 20 names.

One popular study looked at the volatility, or fluctuations, of a portfolio's investment return, and related it to the number of stocks in the portfolio. Table 13 displays the results by presenting the relationship between the number of stocks in a portfolio and the overall risk of the portfolio.

For example, if you hold just four randomly selected NYSE stocks in your portfolio, you have reduced your investment risk — compared to just holding one stock — by 64%. If you hold six randomly selected stocks, you have reduced your investment risk by 70%. In other words, the risk reduction from holding just a few (randomly selected) names in your portfolio declines exponentially. From a different perspective, the benefit from holding 10 stocks, compared to 20, is a minimal (81% – 76% =) 5% reduction in concentration risk.

The lesson in all of this is quite clear. First, concentrating your portfolio in just one or two names is quite dangerous, independently of how optimistic you are about the companies' prospects, or how large the companies happen to be. Second, having 50 stocks in your portfolio won't protect or insulate you from periodic market meltdowns. Diversification can help you, but only up to a point. It can never eliminate the risk–return tradeoff that forms the basis of investing. Third, understand why diversification is essential: It eliminates diversifiable risk without reducing expected return. This benefit alone makes diversification indispensable.

Longevity Insurance: A Product Whose Time Has Come?

23

With the Queen Mother recently passing away at age 101, I myself have started to wonder about seeing triple digits on the cake during my lifetime. Indeed, the demographers and actuaries at Statistics Canada don't like projecting *that* far into the future, but, according to them, a recently retired Canadian female (male) has a 19% (8%) chance of reaching age 95. That's 30 years of leisure, mind you. For a workaholic like myself, it actually sounds like 30 years of hell — but I hope to learn how to play (and enjoy) golf by the time I retire.

It appears that a large segment of our aging population will be spending more time during retirement than in their working years dreaming about their advanced years. Health and quality-of-life issues aside, will you be able to afford the possibility of such a long retirement?

Don't get me wrong. This is not another preachy piece on the virtues of pre-retirement *savings*, fully topped-up RRSPs and the right mutual fund so you can retire with a nest egg that will feed a tribe. Rather, my concerns are at the opposite end of the lifecycle and the never-ending doubt that you are *spending* too much of it.

This is a bigger problem than you think. No matter how old you are, you will always be worried about spending too much. In the back of your mind you will be wondering, "what if I have five, 10 or even 15 years to go?" Taking this logical flow to its extreme, you will never be willing to spend that last dollar. Everybody dies with leftovers! Sure, your kids and estate lawyer (and perhaps even you) might appreciate bequests, but you must admit that there is a certain inefficiency in consistently depriving yourself today, on the odds there is a tomorrow.

While we all crave life, the fear of outliving our money may lead some to ask: Will I live too long? This is a crucial question — and worry — during retirement, because, should your money run out before death, it is unlikely that you will be able to generate additional funds, due to the physical limitations of old age.

Stated alternatively, the money you've saved up for retirement is *all there is*, and it must be carefully allocated to consumption over retirement. But there are two risks: the risk of outliving your money, and the risk of under-consuming, and unnecessarily leaving a large bequest to beneficiaries. Worries about money can wreck a well-deserved retirement. What can the individual investor do to overcome these worries? In an earlier chapter we looked at assets and investments, in this chapter we will look at insurance.

There are a number of ways to address the worry of outliving your money. First, you can be ultra-cautious, and only consume what you must. As mentioned earlier, this will greatly reduce the risk of outliving your money, but is inefficient, as in all likelihood the caution will result in a large bequest to beneficiaries. Of the two risks: outliving your money, or leaving too much money, we'd all prefer to leave too much money rather than to outlive it; hence, some caution is in order. But the inefficiency associated with leaving too much money suggests that being ultra-cautious is not optimal.

Second, you can make a deal with family members, such as your children. The deal would work as follows: Your children agree to support you after a specified age, such as 75, for example. In return you agree to provide a bequest to your children should you die before age 75.

Clearly, such an arrangement is not for everyone. Many individuals would react negatively to the lack of independence associated with having to rely on others for support. Further, the strategy is risky: What will you do if your children back out of the deal, or face a financial crisis, such as personal bankruptcy, making them unable to provide the agreed-upon assistance? Finally, many of us would be uncomfortable with being supported by our children, due to the fear of being perceived as a burden — you definitely don't want your children looking forward to your death (at any level) because of the release of the financial obligation of support it provides.

Is there a third option? One that provides insurance against living too long, without involving your family?

The answer is, yes. (Although I would like to see better-designed products to manage longevity risk.) This type of insurance goes by the better-known moniker of immediate annuities (IA). The way they work is that in exchange for a lump-sum payment to an insurance company you are guaranteed to receive a fixed payment for the rest of your natural life — no matter how long you actually live!

For example, you may choose to purchase an immediate annuity at the age of 65. You invest $100,000 with your financial institution. In return, the financial institution agrees to pay you a fixed payment of $650 every month, regardless of market rates, and regardless of how long you live. Should you live until the age of 127, the financial institution will continue paying the fixed payment until that time.

But should you die at 68, your beneficiaries do not receive a refund.

Longevity insurance or IA allows retirees to stop worrying about whether they will outlive their money — as long as they are alive, they are assured of the fixed payment. This permits retirees to budget carefully for the future, and spend their money on trips or presents for their grandkids — worry free. Most retirees will also leave a nest egg outside of the fixed annuity, for unexpected cash needs, and to use as a bequest to beneficiaries upon death.

"How can the life insurance company afford to offer life annuities?" you asked. Well, I discuss life annuities in an academic paper (see Milevsky, 2001b), but here is the nutshell version.

I'll describe how life annuities work, but first a bit of background. In theory, life insurance companies provide two basic services — life insurance and life annuities — that are symmetric opposites. The basic principle of life insurance is that in exchange for small monthly payments, the insurance company guarantees a large benefit upon your death. Life annuities, on the other hand, essentially provide protection against living too long: In exchange for one large payment now, the insurance company guarantees a small, but steady, monthly benefit until your demise. Traditionally, life insurance is acquired early in the human lifecycle to protect your loved ones, while annuities are purchased during the golden years to protect yourself.

Hence, while by life insurance the insurance company is hoping you'll live longer, by life annuities the insurance company is hoping you'll die earlier — at least from a financial perspective.

Here's a question I'm often asked: Are life annuities a good investment? My answer is, no, not at a young age. But eventually, yes. The reasons for this are as follows. First, financial institutions charge for expenses and transaction costs, such as marketing and broker fees. While they don't specifically request you pay an up-front fee for these purposes, the fees are implicit in the monthly benefit you receive. Second, life annuities are illiquid: It's difficult, if not impossible, to roll back the transaction should your life situation change.

But even though life annuities aren't great investments, that doesn't mean you shouldn't purchase them. Life annuities are more than simply investments; more important, they are insurance. And like other insurance products, such as life insurance or home insurance, we don't purchase life annuities for their investment characteristics, but for their risk-reduction characteristics. After all, why do we purchase insurance in the first place? As I explain in another chapter in this text, we purchase insurance for protection. A sensible individual recognizes that insurance isn't a good investment, but protection is.

But if we buy life annuities for their insurance qualities, what exactly are we trying to insure against? As explained earlier, we are trying to protect ourselves against the possibility of outliving our money. But if so, life annuities are an imperfect product. After all, there is little likelihood that we will run out of money in the first 10 years of retirement, for example. Instead, the risk is greatest should we be lucky enough to live to unexpectedly old age, such as over 90. But if we are trying to avoid running out of money at age 90, why do we need to have fixed benefits at age 65? In other words, given that life annuities are not good investments, but are useful as protection, shouldn't we target the protection to those years of retirement where it's really needed?

Ideally, if I were running the annuity department at my local insurance company, I would design a product (and try to convince the Canada Customs and Revenue Agency to tax it properly) that you purchase

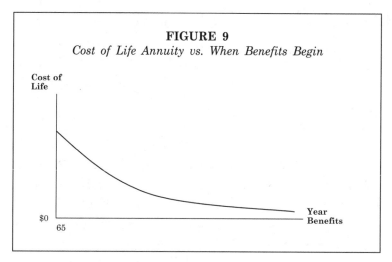

FIGURE 9

Cost of Life Annuity vs. When Benefits Begin

at retirement, but that only starts paying — indexed to inflation — at age 90, or 95. I call this longevity insurance with a deductible. The consumption risk of the first few years you can manage yourself. But then, if you live much longer, the insurance kicks in. If you do the math, you will pay mere cents on the dollar for this type of product, and the fear of having to eat cat food in your centenarian years should evaporate. As presented in Figure 9, there is an inverse relationship between the year the life annuity kicks in, and the cost.

To sum, the purpose of longevity insurance is to allow retirees to relax without having to worry about outliving their money. Life annuities are not a good investment, but are desirable for the protection they provide. It would be ideal if financial institutions offered longevity insurance products targeted to the years of retirement when the risk of outliving one's money is the greatest — the latter years. Regardless, financial planning would be incomplete without considering life annuities upon retirement.

Hedge Funds: Do They Belong in Your Portfolio?

24

The current buzzword among my MBA students and the finance intelligentsia is hedge funds. Indeed, just when George Soros, Michael Steinhart and other legendary money gladiators are leaving the capital market's coliseum, the Canadian public has developed a newfound appreciation for them.

Unfortunately, the generic term hedge fund is being used — and much abused — to describe almost any investment category that isn't a plain stock or a bond. So what are hedge funds, how do they work and, more important, should you own any?

Well, first some history. Hedge funds came into being in 1949, when money manager and part-time *Fortune* columnist Alfred W. Jones developed the idea of short selling stocks that appeared overvalued, in conjunction with long positions (i.e., buying stocks) that were undervalued.

For the novice, short selling means borrowing stocks from your broker and then selling them, hoping that you can buy them back — and returning the stocks to their rightful owner — once their price declines. Think of it as borrowing your next-door neighbour's brand new lawnmower, then selling it to your neighbour down the street, and waiting until they go on sale at Canadian Tire so you can buy an identical one and return it to the original owner. If things work out, you will make a nice profit. If the lawnmower never goes on sale or, worse, if the price increases, you will eventually have to cover your losses.

As unsavoury as this activity sounds, with financial instruments it's perfectly legal and done regularly. In fact, believe it or not, this type of activity actually makes markets function better, and can reduce the overall risk of your portfolio.

The theory behind hedge funds is that by simultaneously combining long and short positions the fund will make money in both bull and bear markets. Or, at the very least, they will not lose as much in rapidly falling markets. Indeed, most (properly classified) hedge funds have a nice property, which the propeller-heads with Ph.D.'s call "zero beta". This is akin to the Holy Grail of modern financial alchemy.

Beta is a measure of the extent to which portfolio returns move in conjunction with stock market returns, and can be perceived as the portfolio's sensitivity to changes in the market.

A beta of one suggests that the portfolio returns move in perfect conjunction with the market: a 5% negative return on the market is associated with a 5% negative return on the portfolio. A beta greater than one suggests that while the portfolio moves in conjunction with the market, the portfolio is riskier than the market. Hence, if an event causes market returns to jump by 4%, the same event will cause a portfolio with beta greater than one to jump by even more. Figure 10 below is an example of a portfolio with a beta greater than one. The broken line is the market return. The other line represents the portfolio returns. As we can see, the portfolio returns are much more sensitive to positive and negative events than the market returns.

A beta between zero and one suggests that the portfolio is less sensitive than the market, but moves in conjunction. A negative beta suggests that the

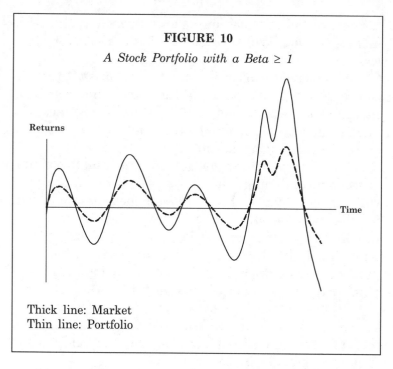

FIGURE 10

A Stock Portfolio with a Beta ≥ 1

Thick line: Market
Thin line: Portfolio

portfolio is negatively correlated with the market; hence, positive market returns are associated with negative portfolio returns and vice versa.

But hedge funds aim for zero beta. A true zero beta asset earns investment returns that are completely uncorrelated with the general market. The zero beta ship sails calmly through the perfect storm without being influenced by the turbulent sea around it. That's not to say that hedge fund returns do not fluctuate. They certainly do! But they fluctuate less than, and should march to a drummer different than does the overall market. And that's good, because you want them to zig when the rest of your portfolio zags.

In the past, these investments were limited to sophisticated players with a high net worth. Today, these products have gone mainstream, and there is a strong case to be made for sprinkling your Aunt Martha's RRSP portfolio with the risk-reducing effects of hedge funds.

However, there are a number of reasons to think twice before including hedge funds in your portfolio.

First, some argue that other alternative investments are preferable to hedge funds as risk-reduction tools. For example, a recent study by Franklin Edwards and Mustafa Caglayan in the *Journal of Portfolio Management* suggests that commodity funds generally offer better downside protection than hedge funds (see Edwards and Caglayan, 2001).

The study provides empirical evidence based on hedge fund versus commodity fund performance during bull and bear markets. The authors find that commodity funds have higher returns in bear markets than hedge funds, and are negatively correlated with stocks in bear markets. Hedge funds, on the other hand, generally perform poorly during bear markets, and have higher correlation with stock markets in bear markets than in bull markets.

Hence, commodity funds do a better job of reducing risk. After all, the purpose of risk reduction is to dampen the negative impact of bear markets. The higher correlation between hedge funds and stock markets during bear markets suggests that during the periods where risk reduction is most necessary, hedge funds may not perform adequately.

Second, many investment products that are masquerading under the title of hedge funds are really speculative funds that are buying and selling Estonian bonds, Argentinean debt, and baskets of West African currencies. There is nothing wrong with taking a flier on these instruments, but there is nothing hedged about them either. And the volatility can be mind numbing.

Remember, though, the turnover on these funds is quite high, which means you will face a large tax bill on a regular basis, unless the funds are held in an RRSP/RESP or similar tax sheltered plan.

In sum, I encourage you to consider including some non-traditional asset categories in your investment portfolio so that you can hedge (or mitigate) some of the fluctuations that are due to the general co-movement of stocks and bonds. Placing some non-traditional investments side-by-side with well-known assets can have the effect of a shot of whisky at the end of a hard day's work. They both can take the edge off a harsh world. But, you don't want to go overboard with hedge funds (or the whisky, for that matter).

Furthermore, other alternative investments, such as commodity funds, may provide even better risk-reduction effects. Finally, you might want to ensure that the benefits associated with including the hedge fund in your portfolio justify the investment fees, such as the high MERs associated with hedge funds.

Trading Day and Night

25

It's 2:00 am and you are having a tough time sleeping. What should you do? Have a glass of hot milk? Watch some TV? Read a book? Well, how about trading stocks? Yes, you can now log on to your favourite online broker and load up on some Nortel or dump your JDS, all this while watching the infomercial for the Abdomenizer. Welcome to the world of night trading.

Up to a year or so ago, after-hours trading, as it officially is called, was only available to professional institutional traders who wanted to move large blocks of stock. Today, the after-hours market is open to the small fry — although activity is heavily concentrated in the 4:00 pm to 6:30 pm and 8:00 am to 9:30 am time slots — thanks to the creation of Electronic Communications Networks, better known as ECNs.

As you might already know, during the day, orders to buy and sell stock are most likely to be processed by middleman firms known as market makers, broker dealers or specialists. At night, the ECNs take over, and they don't sleep.

How do they work? Well, at a simple level, ECNs are the stock market equivalent of eBay, where you can auction (buy and sell) your favourite stocks, for the best available price. You don't have to wait days for a response — as you might have to do on eBay — and in most cases you will find an offer within seconds. Also, instead of you personally logging on to this system, your online broker routes your trade to the anonymous ECN, which then does the auctioning for you. So Edward who is buying in Edmonton doesn't know that it is Tommy who is selling in Toronto. The anonymity is quite helpful to traders who want to (quite legitimately) obscure their positions and intentions.

Despite all the high-tech wizardry behind the ECNs, trades cannot take place unless there are enough traders. For the system to work — or, as the economists would say, for markets to clear — you need enough people on both sides of the market. But make no mistake about it, these ECNs are the future of stock trading, both day and night.

Of course, not all trades are routed through ECNs. Some broker dealers do operate at night, and many popular stocks are cross-listed on other exchanges and trade overseas.

But the retail trades you place on your favourite OnLineBroker.com are virtually guaranteed to end up at the ECN. And, there are many available ECNs to which your online broker can route your trades. The different ones operate under cute names like Archipelago, Instinet and Island. But, as long as the central computer is turned on, your stocks can be auctioned.

How efficient is this for the small investor? Some people who trade overnight have no choice: For one reason or another, they must trade at that time. But for many overnight traders, they can easily wait until normal daytime trading is available. Given the choice between trading while the markets are open, or after hours, which should these investors choose?

To evaluate whether ECNs are efficient for the small investor, we have to consider the costs associated with these trades, and whether stock prices are more volatile overnight.

TABLE 14		
What Is the Difference between Day and Night?		
Trades on NASDAQ and NYSE		
	Day *(9:30 am–4:05 pm)*	*Night* *(all other times)*
Percent of Total Trades	99.2%	0.8%
Average Trade Size (USD)	$52,000	$140,000
Bid–Ask Spread Cost	0.5%	1.0%

Source: M.J. Barclay and T. Hendershott, University of Rochester, <www.afterhourstrading.com>.

Well, in a recent (and landmark) study of the differences between day and night trading, Professors M. Barclay and T. Hendershott at the University of Rochester examined six months' worth of minute-by-minute data on stock trades made during the day and at night. That's a huge amount of data to analyze! To analyze all of the data, the study was performed using advanced statistical software.

They document a few important facts. Not surprisingly, the majority of the volume in stock trading is still being done during the regular exchange hours of 9:30 am to 4:05 pm. Less than 1% of the total NASDAQ and NYSE trades made in any given 24-hour period are placed in after-hours trading.

For example, if 45,000 trades are made on a given stock in a 24-hour period, on average less than 1%, or 450 trades, are made after hours — not a large amount at all.

While the number of trades made after hours is small, the size of the trades that do take place is relatively large. The study finds that the average size of a trade placed after hours is approximately three times larger than the average trade during the day. Clearly, the night trades are not buying and selling single lots.

In addition, the report documents much higher *price volatility* and larger *price impact costs*, as well as lower *liquidity* associated with after-hours trading.

"Volatility" refers to the degree to which the price of a stock fluctuates during the period of observation. Note that a stock can be considered volatile even if its price remains unchanged between the beginning and the end of the period.

"Price impact costs" refer to costs associated with executing a trade swiftly. The price impact costs will be reflected in the bid–ask spread as well as the dealer's price concessions.

"Liquidity" refers to the ease, and cost, with which assets can be bought or sold. For example, real estate or art market investments are relatively illiquid relative to stocks on the market, in terms of transaction costs associated with each trade. Similarly, we can compare the liquidity associated with any two stocks, using measures such as the bid–ask spread.

What all this means to you personally is that, despite the cheap sounding $20 commission, once you impute the increased volatility, larger price impact costs, and lower liquidity associated with after-hours trading, it costs you more to trade after hours.

The study also notes the following interesting observation: Unlike daytime trading, after-hours trades are completed using distilled information and are thereby associated more with significant price discovery (prices move as a result of information, not just noise).

But quite telling is that Professors Barclay and Hendershott conclude their exhaustive study with the following remarks: "We see few benefits to bringing after-hours trading to individuals."

So, if you happen to wake up in the middle of the night with a sudden urge to re-jig your small portfolio, you might want to wait until breakfast time. On the other hand, if you are dumping that $1 million holding in Cisco, and you don't want the market to know who you are, midnight darkness might be the perfect cover.

Housing: Investment or Consumption?

26

My wife Edna and I have been searching for a new house for the last six months. We currently rent a small condominium apartment, and after examining real estate prices in Toronto, I'm predicting our search might go on for quite a while.

Not that this is a bad thing, mind you. Although we are currently paying rent, we are saving money on property taxes and maintenance for every month that we don't actually own a house. Furthermore, it appears that investment returns from housing real estate over the long run are not expected to be great either. Indeed, while some regions and neighbourhoods have done quite well, for the most part Canadian home ownership has performed poorly as an asset over the past decade, when properly compared to other investment opportunities.

But we face a lot of pressure when faced with the choice to buy or rent. You may feel desperate to purchase a house after the barbecue you suffered through last weekend, during which your cousin Morris regaled you with the story of how the house he purchased for $250,000, just four months ago, is now worth $400,000. Not only that, but Morris claims that interest rates "have never been better". You may be thinking about the 13% you lost in the stock market during the past year, and may resolutely decide that the time has come to purchase a home. Indeed, evidence suggests that as stock returns decline, consumers may move into housing or other durable goods (see Runkle, 1988). This makes sense. Given the choice between high investment returns and buying a house, many investors would prefer to stay in the markets. But when markets are performing poorly, many investors perceive housing as a safer investment than the stock market, especially if risk-free investments don't offer particularly high returns.

So what's the correct decision? Should you bite the bullet and purchase a home, or should you keep your savings invested in your investment portfolio, and keep on paying rent?

Indeed, there are many benefits associated with home ownership, such as the sense of stability and freedom. Indeed, the emotional appeal of home ownership leads some to treat home hunting and the eventual purchase in the same way as dating and marriage, respectively. However, the purchase of real estate is, fundamentally, an investment.

The first argument in support of caution is that while housing prices can change dramatically, historical evidence suggests that when properly measured the return on investment for Canadian homeowners is not as stupendous as you might think. Canadian investments in home ownership have not performed that well over the past decade, relative to other investment opportunities.

To analyze this issue, I used data compiled by Royal LePage that tracks housing prices, taxes, and rent to compare the after-tax return from $100,000 "invested" in a house in Coquitlam, B.C., Markham, Ont., or Boucherville, Que., to the same $100,000 invested in stocks and T-Bills. I made sure to include the rent that you "save" when you own your own home, as part of the "return" from the real estate investment. In other words, a proper calculation of the investment returns from real estate must include the imputed savings from not having to rent as well as the obvious expenses for maintenance, taxes and insurance.

To start off, the nice thing about housing real estate as an investment is that any capital gains on your principal residence are exempt from income taxes. Your equity portfolio growth, however, is subject to capital gains taxes, and your T-Bill interest income is taxed as well.

But, it appears that this advantage does not amount to much. Indeed, over the decade spanning 1991 to 2001, $100,000 invested in the TSE 300 grew into $224,000, and $100,000 invested in low-risk six-month T-Bills grew to $152,000; both figures are after tax. And, as Figure 11 indicates, the growth of the housing investments did not match that of the TSE 300. The $100,000 housing investment in Coquitlam was worth $178,060, in Markham it was worth $189,970 and in Boucherville it was worth $160,290. While the results may not apply to other locations and time periods, they do suggest that the return potential associated with housing investments is exaggerated.

Of course, equity prices are more volatile than housing prices. Hence, one might argue that the TSE 300 received higher returns due to the risk–return tradeoff, and therefore comparing housing prices to the TSE 300 on a face-to-face basis is unfair. However, even after adjusting for risk, only the investment in a house in Markham approaches the volatility-adjusted TSE 300 equivalent growth.

How do I adjust for volatility? There are a number of methods of doing so. One measure of return that is adjusted for risk is the Sharpe ratio. The Sharpe ratio permits us to compare investments with different levels of volatility, through standardizing returns using their respective volatility levels.

In the face of such evidence, many homeowners argue that by purchasing a house, as opposed to rent-

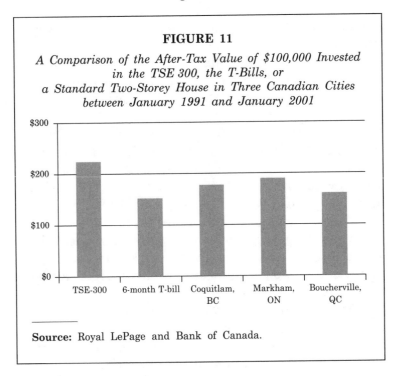

FIGURE 11

*A Comparison of the After-Tax Value of $100,000 Invested
in the TSE 300, the T-Bills, or
a Standard Two-Storey House in Three Canadian Cities
between January 1991 and January 2001*

Source: Royal LePage and Bank of Canada.

ing, they are able to borrow money that they couldn't access otherwise.

But then again, you can always buy stocks and mutual funds on margin, albeit not with a 20-to-1 leverage ratio and with CMHC insurance. Those investments are liquid, they don't have closing costs, deposits, or 6% commissions, and I certainly don't have to shovel the snow or mow the lawn on my mutual fund.

Some ownership advocates argue that when you pay rent to your landlord, you are "throwing" the money away, but when you finance your house with a mortgage, you are "redeeming" a piece of your house each and every month. But I challenge these folks to look at how much mortgage interest they are actually paying the bank, and how much truly goes towards the principal of the home.

Yes, in an inflationary environment, your rent might increase. But then again, so might your mortgages payments, property taxes, maintenance fees, etc.

Others might wonder: Is the TSE 300 or the T-Bill rate the proper benchmark for housing comparison? In fact, if you invested internationally — and leveraged with tax deductible interest — your after-tax returns would have been much higher. Are Coquitlam, Markham and Boucherville good proxies for what your neighbourhood is like? In fact, these are relatively safe-investment neighbourhoods. With many others, you would have been lucky to get your money back.

Another argument in support of caution when considering an investment in a home is that the investment is completely undiversified. If you were considering an investment in art, would you invest all of your assets in a single piece of art, or would you diversify among different pieces? Like we discussed previously in another chapter, a fundamental principle of investing is, "Don't put all your eggs in one basket". Investment research has demonstrated that while there is a tradeoff between risk and return, this tradeoff only applies to risk that cannot be diversified away. Hence, only a highly diversified portfolio maximizes return per unit of risk.

Most families invest a considerable proportion, if not all, of their assets into the home purchase. Further, they leverage this undiversified investment heavily. Hence, family wealth is almost entirely a function of the worth of a single home. Potential returns aside, I am constantly puzzled by individuals (e.g., my wife) who would never dare invest a large fraction of their financial wealth in a single stock, or asset class, yet they are quite willing to sink their life savings into a couple of tons of lifeless bricks and mortar.

Sure, financial scholars have demonstrated that you get compensated, in the very long run, for taking some chances with your money, but this only applies to risk that cannot be diversified away. In other words, if you want to invest in housing — and it might be a wonderful diversification strategy, given today's markets — buy a real estate mutual fund that holds a collection of properties, don't take a chance on just one.

Okay, I agree that the pros and cons are numerous, and I could go on debating the buy-versus-rent issue for days. Here's my motto, "housing is consumption, not investment", but go explain that to the kids.

To summarize, the final decision to purchase a home, and the decision regarding the size of the home, requires the investor to weigh the benefits and costs associated with the investment. Some benefits are intangible — such as the sense of ownership, the sense of not having to deal with a landlord, and the sense of stability. In no way should the potential homeowner discount these intangible benefits. However, the homeowner must evaluate how much is forgone, in terms of alternative opportunities. How much is the decision to invest an additional $150,000 in a home really costing, in terms of return and diversification? Without such an honest evaluation, the investment in a home may prove to be a poor investment indeed.

Car Leases and Hidden Options

27

My 1991 Ford Topaz is on its deathbed. I naïvely bought her brand new, back in the summer of 1991, with about 2% down and 98% borrowed from Ford Credit. It took 48 monthly payments of precisely $367 to actually own her, not to mention the thousands of dollars and hundreds of hours of maintenance costs during the last few years she has been under geriatric care. I've enjoyed owning my car, but now it's time for me to bite the bullet and buy another one.

How do I finance her replacement? I have my eye on a swanky black German Mercedes Benz, which I can't afford to own for many reasons. But whichever car I choose, should I lease the car, or should I borrow money to buy the car, as I did back in 1991?

Well, this time around I'm not going to make the same mistake. In my situation, leasing is the superior strategy. This may shock many of my readers, who may feel that leasing is a fool's game. So let me explain my thinking behind my decision to lease my next car rather than purchase it outright.

You see, leasing is akin to renting a car for 36 months, after which you return the car to the vendor. You own nothing, and owe nothing. If, on the other hand, you borrow money to buy the car, you will still make monthly payments, but you will actually own the car once the payments have been completed.

At first glance, the choice seems obvious. Why would you rent something, if you can make the exact same payments and own it? Surely the residual value of the car makes up for the higher payments associated with purchasing a car versus renting?

That was my erroneous thinking the first time around.

The process is a bit more complicated. All else being equal, you will definitely be making lower monthly payments on a car lease compared to a car loan. That's because when you lease a car, you are only acquiring the next 36 months of its life. When you buy a car, you are getting the car for the rest of its life. This asymmetry between the life of the relationship for each alternative, buying or leasing, is the reason why so many otherwise sophisticated investors throw their hands up when faced with the choice to buy or lease. It's difficult enough to choose between two similar options. How do we go about choosing between what appears to be two completely different alternatives?

So, here is a simplified way to think about the choice. Let's begin by stating the obvious.

First, if you are the type who buys a car and then drives it until it dies, then you are probably better off borrowing money to buy the car, as opposed to leasing. After all, you know that you will be using the car over the long run, and have no intention of selling it until it dies — like my Topaz. Once your payments are finished, you face no further financial obligation.

In contrast, if you savour the feeling of driving a brand new car every few years, you don't intend to have a long-term relationship with the car. In this case, you should probably lease. These issues are a matter of consumer taste, and have nothing to do with the financial economics of leasing.

Second, if you own a small business, and acquire the car as part of the business, there may be tax implications associated with the buy-versus-lease choice. In this case, consult your local tax professional. The tax implications may well make the decision for you.

But let's say you are unsure as to how long you intend to keep the car, face no tax implications, and want to base your decision solely on the underlying finance. From a financial perspective, how do we go about deciding whether to buy or lease?

To begin our analysis, you should be aware of an issue that is less obvious than, but equally important to, the payments you make every month. When you lease a car, your monthly payments will depend not only on the current interest rates — the higher the interest rates, the more you pay — they also depend on something called the "purchase option".

Every lease contract contains the right, but not the obligation, to purchase the car at the end of the lease for a pre-determined fixed price. The lessor — the entity that leased the car to you — has the obligation to let you purchase the car at the pre-determined price, should you wish to exercise your option.

The right embedded in the purchase option is very similar to a well-known derivative security called a call option, that is traded on options markets. If you remember, a call option is an agreement between two parties. One party has the right to purchase a pre-specified underlying security or asset at a pre-specified price some time in the future. The second party is obligated to sell the underlying security or asset at the pre-specified price, should the option holder wish to exercise the option. In return, the second party receives an up-front fee, which is a function of a number of factors, such as the current price, the pre-specified price, and interest rates.

The first party will only choose to exercise the right if the pre-specified price is less than the market price. After all, in that case, the first party can simply exercise the right and turn around and sell the underlying security or asset at a higher price. Should the pre-specified price be lower than the market price, the first party will not take advantage of the right, for why bother to do so, when the underlying security or asset can be purchased for less on the market.

For example, you might make lease payments of $400 per month for 36 months, at the end of which you have the option to purchase the car for $20,000 or walk away.

If, in 36 months, the market value of the car happens to be greater than $20,000, you might want to exercise your right to buy the car for $20,000 — even if you have no intention to keep it — and then turn around and sell it for its higher market value. If, on the other hand, the value of the car is less than $20,000, you simply walk away from the lease.

This $20,000 number, which I will call a strike price, has a substantial impact on your monthly lease payments. Indeed, the leasing company doesn't like to give out "free options", and therefore the lower the strike price, the higher your monthly payments will be.

The higher the strike price of the purchase option, the less valuable is the option to purchase the car, and the lower your monthly payments should be. So, if you have no interest in ever purchasing this car, push the strike price as high as you possibly can.

Notice from the simplified Table 15 that even if the leasing company insists on a 50% strike price — which is extreme — you are still paying less than half of what you would have paid by purchasing the car.

So, let me get back to my original question. Should you lease or buy? Well, although it certainly

	TABLE 15		
		Buy	*Lease*
	Strike Price (a.k.a. Residual Value)		
		36 Monthly Payments	
100%	$20,000	$617.5	$116.7
85%	$17,000	$617.5	$191.8
70%	$14,000	$617.5	$266.9
60%	$12,000	$617.5	$317.0
50%	$10,000	$617.5	$367.1
35%	$ 7,000	$617.5	$442.2

Initial price (a.k.a. Capitalized Cost) of vehicle is $20,000.
Ignores taxes, licence fees and destination charges.
No down payment, with 7% p.a. nominal interest rate.

_____

Source: Author calculations.

depends on your taste for new cars, I'm going with a lease this time. As you can see from the table, if I can push the buyback price to about 70%, I'll be paying less than half in monthly lease payments, compared to the cost of owning. Furthermore, I avoid those awful maintenance costs that are likely to kick in just as the lease is about to expire.

One thing is certain, when you are pondering the buy-versus-lease decision, it's a good idea to dust off those old high school calculus books — or bring along that quaint friend of yours — since the skills will sure come in handy when dealing with these confusing sales pitches.

You Are Wealthier Than You Think

My sister-in-law recently lost her job as a programmer for a high-tech company that went belly-up. The sad thing is that her employee stock options are now worthless as well, which adds further insult to injury.

The poor employees of the disastrous Enron Corporation in Texas are suffering an even greater calamity. A large portion of their 401(k) personal pension fund was invested in the near worthless company stock, and the recent number of unemployed within the same region will likely depress real estate values as well — a double whammy.

While my heart aches for them, I believe they engaged in very poor financial planning, by not diversifying — and by hedging — their human capital and financial capital.

Financial capital is the sum of your liquid wealth, such as savings and real estate, minus your debts. The more abstract human capital is the *present value* of all the wages, salary and commissions you expect to earn during the course of your working life. You can't really touch, feel or see human capital, but like a reserve deep under the oil wells of Alberta, it's definitely there and worth something.

During the course of your working life, you will convert human capital into financial capital. Your total capital, which is your *true* net worth, is defined as the sum of your human capital and financial capital.

For example, consider an individual who has just completed medical school. The individual has no financial assets, and in fact owes various creditors $45,000 — money the individual borrowed to finance the medical degree. Superficially, the individual might be perceived as "poor", because of the poor state of his or her finances. However, because of the earning power associated with a medical degree, the human capital of this individual is huge, well into hundreds of thousands, if not millions, of dollars. The *true* net worth of this individual, therefore, is much greater than the value of the individual's bank account.

Of course, computing the value of human capital is not a trivial exercise — compared to adding up your financial worth — since you have to project your future earnings, and express the value of these future earnings in today's dollars. Remember, the dollar you earn 20 years from now is worth much less than a dollar in the bank today, even if we assume zero inflation.

The process through which we express the value of future earnings in today's dollars is designated *discounting*. To discount future earnings, we multiply them by a value termed the *discount factor*. The discount factor is similar to an exchange rate. Except, instead of converting Euros to Canadian dollars, we convert, for example, 2020 dollars into 2003 dollars.

The discount factor is inversely related to two factors: time and interest rates. Hence, the higher the interest rates, the lower the discount factor, and the less the future dollar is worth today. Similarly, the longer the time until the future earnings take place, the lower the discount factor. Therefore, a different discount factor is specified for every point in time at which cash flows are received in the future.

The challenge is deciding upon the correct discount factor to use when discounting those cash flows associated with future earnings.

However, regardless of the method you choose and the numbers you use, one thing is surprising. The value of your human capital is much higher than the value of your financial capital, until quite late in life. Indeed, using data from Statistics Canada about the financial assets and earnings of Canadians, I created a rough picture of the relative magnitude of the two forms of capital.

As you can see from Figure 12, for the average Canadian, like myself, between the ages of 25 and 44, 90% or more of total (human + financial) capital is locked up in human capital, and only 10% is financial capital. The reason, again, is that I have approximately 30 more working years ahead of me, and the present value of those wages far exceeds my current financial capital.

So, now that I have convinced you that human capital is a substantial part of total capital on the balance sheet of ME Inc., the important and practical side is to integrate this "asset" into an overall financial plan, and make sure the total capital is properly diversified.

What do I mean by "properly diversified"? First, let me remind you of the diversification effect, which reduces diversifiable risk without reducing expected return. It occurs when investors increase the number of different investments in their portfolio. Most important, the diversification effect is the strongest when some investments in the portfolio "zig" while others "zag".

Since our personal portfolio consists of both financial and human capital, we optimize our portfolio through ensuring that it is properly diversified. For those holding their retirement savings as investment in the company they work for, their portfolio is poorly

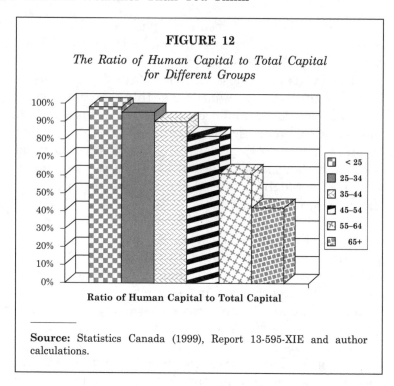

FIGURE 12

*The Ratio of Human Capital to Total Capital
for Different Groups*

Ratio of Human Capital to Total Capital

Source: Statistics Canada (1999), Report 13-595-XIE and author calculations.

diversified. Clearly, both components of their total capital are sensitive to the same underlying factors. Therefore, when their human capital performs poorly, so does their financial capital, and vice versa.

Similarly, your job and your investments should not be identical. If you are in the automobile industry, keep your investments out of the industry. That way, should a crisis befall the industry and you lose your job, at least your financial assets won't decrease in value as well.

A natural question follows. *Is your human capital closer to a bond fund, or an equity fund?*

Well, if you have a stable job with a predictable income — for example, a tenured professor, or government employee — then your human capital is very much in the bond category. Hence, your financial capital should be heavily tilted towards equities. On the other hand, if you work in a volatile and unpredictable industry, then you already have a substantial allocation to a type of risky equity, and your financial capital should be tilted towards more bonds.

Unfortunately, in practice, total capital is concentrated in employment, industries and sectors. And what is lacking is integrated financial planning. The key is to look at your total asset allocation, and not just the — much smaller — financial asset allocation.

Remember, you are the CFO (Chief Financial Officer) of ME Inc., and the left-hand side of your balance sheet is much larger than you think. The rules of diversification apply to more than simply your money.

Estates, Death and Taxes: To Insure or Not?

The recent death of a distant aunt of mine reminded me, once again, that the two inevitabilities of life — death and taxes — are strongly intertwined.

As you probably know, the tax implications of your death can hardly be exaggerated.

For the most part, there is an irksome "deemed disposition" rule which states that your executor, or whoever is responsible for filing your final tax return, must treat all your assets "as if" they were sold on your date of death. And thus, if you had any assets that appreciated in value since they were acquired, you will be liable for income (or capital gains) taxes. Likewise, unless your RRSP or RRIF was transferred to your spouse (or certain dependants in particular circumstances), the tax authorities will de-register the tax-sheltered pension, and tax all the money in the account.

All of these can add up to quite a hefty tax bill, which is why it is very common to see life insurance sold, solely for the purpose of paying your taxes upon death. The death benefit is usually tax free and, if structured properly, can exactly cover the expected tax liability.

For example, let's say you own a cottage. You purchased the cottage in 1975 for $12,000, and it is now valued at $400,000. You wish for the cottage to remain in the family, and you would definitely not want your family to sell it upon your death. But the capital gain on the cottage, ignoring previous capital gain exemptions, is $388,000. The resulting tax bill could be well over $100,000. To pay these taxes, your family may have no choice but to sell the cottage. To avoid the forced sale of it, you can purchase life insurance that pays your beneficiaries an amount upon death approximately equivalent to the expected tax liability.

However, despite its popularity and intuitive appeal, I'm not a fan or advocate of insurance solely for the purpose of hedging against death and taxes. It only makes sense under limited conditions, and for the most part, you will simply be pre-paying your inevitable income taxes. There is no free lunch in this strategy.

Let me explain with the help of some numbers. Assume that you (or more precisely, your estate) are facing a $100,000 tax liability upon your death.

To cover this large and unpleasant liability, you decide to purchase a life insurance (technically, a term-to-100 with no cash value for a healthy male) policy that will pay $100,000 tax free to your estate, spouse or children, upon your death. If you initiate such a policy at age 50, you will pay a constant $1,030 per annum for the rest of your life. If you start at age 60, it will be $2,130, and at age 70 it will be $3,320, per annum, for life. Naturally, the older you are, the greater the probability of death within the next year, the higher the premiums.

Now, as you can see from Table 16, if you start the process at 60, *and* you live for 20 more years to age 80, you will have paid a total of $42,600 in premiums, in exchange for a death benefit of $100,000. The future value of those $42,600 in premiums, had they been invested instead, and at an after-tax rate of 5%, would be $74,000 upon your death at age 80. Please bear with me.

TABLE 16
$100,000 Death Benefit to Cover Expected Taxes

Starting Age	Premium	Percent of Tax Liability You Pre-Pay If You Die at Age				
		75	80	85	90	95
50	$1,030	51.6%	71.9%	97.7%	130.6%	172.7%
60	$2,130	48.3%	74.0%	106.7%	148.6%	202.0%
70	$3,320	19.3%	43.8%	75.2%	115.3%	166.4%

Assumptions: Term-to-100 policy with no cash value, 5% after-tax discount rate, best health male.

Methodology: Future value of premiums at death, divided by face value of policy.

———

Source: N. Charupat, J. Dhaene and M.A. Milevsky, "When is it Optimal to Hedge against Death and Taxes?" Working Paper, Schulich School of Business, 2002.

What this means is that at the assumed death at age 80, you will have pre-paid $74,000 towards the $100,000 you will receive from the insurance company, which you purchased to cover the expected $100,000 tax liability. Therefore, I conclude that in this case, you have pre-paid 74% of your taxes. The remaining 26% will be covered by the insurance company, or more precisely, your neighbour who outlives you.

On its own, this 74% number is not alarming. However, if you, the 60-year-old male, ends up living to age 85, you will have paid the equivalent of 106.7% of the death benefit (a.k.a. expected tax liability). This is because you will have paid a total of $106,700 in (future value of) premiums, and only received $100,000 in return. Note that you actually end up paying more in insurance premiums than they you in death benefits. (One can think of this as an approximately −6.7% total return, above and beyond the 5% interest rate.)

As you can see from the table, the longer you live, the more you will have unnecessarily pre-paid your tax bill and earned a horrendously negative rate of return on your premiums. I call this a tax pre-overpayment strategy.

Now, in general, insurance should not be thought of as a financial investment that earns a high return, but rather as a risk management strategy to protect your dependants and loved ones. Therefore, even though I personally have been paying insurance premiums for the last 10 years, I am quite content with my exceedingly negative rate of return on that particular investment. Indeed, I hope to live a long and healthy life, eventually drop the policy altogether, and thus earn a negative 100% return on my premiums. In financial economic lingo, I am buying life insurance because of the strong risk aversion of my family to losing its sole breadwinner as well as the negative correlation between my human capital and the payoff from the policy.

However, when you are simply trying to cover a certain tax liability and the cash is on hand to pay that liability, it makes little sense to insure against such an event. Naturally, there are exceptions to this rule, and you might use insurance to grow your money in a tax-deferred manner, but that is a separate and distinct strategy from what we are discussing here.

In sum, if you own a very illiquid asset, which you, or your heirs, do not want to sell, *and* they will probably not have the cash on hand to pay the tax liability, then by all means, get some permanent life insurance to cover the tax. However, if the asset is relatively liquid, such as cash, stocks, bonds, mutual funds, or anything sitting in an RRSP or RRIF, then don't bother with insurance. When the inevitable day arrives, they can sell a portion of the financial asset — which is the way Ottawa treats it — and then pay whatever is needed to cover the tax liability. Otherwise, you are simply pre-paying (and possibly overpaying) the tax liability. Hey, look at it this way, if the kids are going to get your leftovers, let them deal with the tax.

Credit Cards and Debit Dilemmas

30

When I was an 18-year-old university freshman, I asked my grandfather to co-sign a credit card application. He declined because he was opposed to credit cards on moral grounds. At the time, I attributed his response to an outdated depression-era mentality to debt, and located a more liberal and younger uncle to sign on the dotted line.

However, whenever the credit card bills arrive in the mail, especially after a festive holiday season, I wonder if perhaps my grandfather had a good point.

Indeed, while interest rates in the economy have plummeted during the last few months, I saw no changes in the rates listed on my credit card statements. And, if I were to carry a balance from month to month — which I hope I never have to do — the interest charged would exceed the investment returns I could ever earn on the best of mutual funds.

In fact, according to Statistics Canada, 38% of Canadians carry a monthly balance on their credit card, and the average balance is approximately $3,000. The interest rates charged range from 9% to 19% per annum on bank cards, and as much as 24% to 29% on retailer plastic.

When I questioned bankers on the apparent lack of sensitivity to falling interest rates, I was told that delinquencies and defaults, which have a large and legitimate impact on the credit card interest rates, have been on the rise due to the faltering economy.

This, paradoxically, feeds into higher credit card rates, even as market interest rates decline. Also, as one of them gruffly pointed out to me, somebody has to pay for the interest-free loan made to all those people, like me, who do pay off their monthly balance on time. The bankers may have a point.

Some are beginning to suggest, however, that we can't place all of the blame for increased delinquencies and defaults on the poor economy. Instead, our society may be changing in fundamental ways, and these changes are leading to increased delinquency and default. For example, there is some empirical evidence that suggests delinquency and bankruptcy are more likely now than they were in years past. In an interesting study published in the *Review of Financial Studies*, the authors argue that, because people today attach less of a stigma to declaring bankruptcy, individuals are more likely to default on their credit card debt (see Gross and Souleles, 2002).

The increased probability of default raises the cost of debt for all of us. After all, the rates that creditors charge can be broken down into risk-free and risky components. The risk-free component is the rate the creditor would charge a borrower who will never default — such as the Canadian government. The risky component is the difference (spread) between the actual rate charged and the risk-free rate. This component of rates compensates the risk creditors face when they lend to borrowers who may default. Note that the rate the creditors *expect* to earn is different than the rate they charge. This is because some borrowers will default, providing the creditors with zero interest, and loss of principal. Hence, don't think that your creditors' lending portfolios are actually earning the rate they charge you!

For example, consider a situation where the risk-free interest rate is 4%. Due to the fear of default on the part of risky borrowers, the financial institution that provided you the credit card charges 23% interest. The 19% spread between the quoted rate and the risk-free rate is to compensate the financial institution for accepting the risk of borrower default as well as other expenses associated with credit cards, such as financing those credit card users who pay their bills promptly. Hence, the actual rate received by the financial institution can be considerably less than 23%.

Indeed, many of the undergraduate students that I teach have no choice *but* to finance their daily consumption and living expenses using this type of credit mechanism. They have no other financial assets to speak of, and are probably carrying hefty student loans as well. I can understand an individual in such a situation accepting sky-high interest rates: they may simply have no other choice. I can also understand why credit card companies charge these individuals such high rates: because of the day-to-day financial existence of many students, they face a high default risk, which justifies high interest rates.

But what is very puzzling to me is that such a large proportion of people who carry a balance on their credit cards (38% of Canadians) have money in their savings accounts (88%), RRSPs (55%), mortgages (35%), vehicle loans (21%), and high-interest consumer debt.

Why is this puzzling?

Well, unlike financial *assets*, where diversification and the motto of "not putting all your eggs in one basket" makes perfect sense, financial liabilities are different. In all likelihood, when you have a collection of financial liabilities, like a car loan, credit debt, department store purchase plan, margin account and a mortgage, etc., you are probably paying a different interest rate on every single one of them. Clearly, any loan that is secured against an asset will have a lower rate.

That's why it makes absolutely no sense to have more than one debt. You should try to have all your debt consolidated, for lack of a better word, into *one* financial liability with the lowest possible interest rate. After all, if you can borrow at a lower rate, why continue to borrow at a higher rate?

For example, consider a situation where you have a credit line available through your bank, whereby you can borrow cash at a low rate of interest (possibly secured against other assets, such as real estate and investments). You also have a $5,000 balance on your credit card. The rate you pay on the credit line is 6%, while the rate you pay on your credit card is 18%. To reduce interest payments, the sensible action to take is to use your credit line to pay down the credit card debt. Then, work to pay down the credit line debt.

Indeed, putting your debts into "silos" only serves to increase the total amount of interest you will pay. After all, what's the point of rapidly paying down your mortgage, when you are running a deficit at twice the interest rate, resulting in a huge credit card balance? Unfortunately, most people figure they should pay down their large debts first, without regard to the actual interest rates charged on the smaller debts.

Table 17 should help illustrate the fallacy in such thinking. The purpose of the table is to specify the actual interest you pay, for different balances and rates. The table considers three rates: a high rate of 21%, a medium rate of 14%, and a low rate of 7%. It looks at four average monthly balances, ranging from $1,000 to $7,000, in increments of $2,000. This table can be used to calculate the actual annual savings you receive by transferring from a higher rate to a lower rate.

For example, if you carry an average monthly balance of $5,000, and are being charged an interest

TABLE 17
What Does Debt Really Cost?

Average Monthly Balance	High Rate 21%	Medium Rate 14%	Low Rate 7%
$1,000	$ 231.44	$ 149.34	$ 72.29
$3,000	$ 694.32	$ 448.03	$216.87
$5,000	$1,157.20	$ 746.71	$361.45
$7,000	$1,620.08	$1,045.39	$506.03

Source: Author calculations.

rate of 21% on your department store or bank credit card, then you are paying approximately $1,157.20 in interest payments each year. Now, if you can shift the debt to your mortgage, for example, at a conservative 7%, then you would reduce the annual payment to $361, which corresponds to a savings of $796. So, even though you might be increasing the size of your mortgage by $5,000, the benefit would be substantial.

The table can also be interpreted in the other direction. If you have $5,000 in an RRSP, earning 7%, for example, and you have a *persistent* $5,000 average monthly balance on your credit card, accruing at 21%, then cashing in the RRSP — ignoring tax for the moment — and paying down the debt would save you $796 per annum. Of course, you would be killing the long-term tax shelter, but this might be the best recourse for habitual credit balances.

Now, I recognize that some shifts are difficult to do. If you've been working hard to pay down your mortgage, you may be very reluctant to increase it again, even if there is a cost savings. I also know individuals who would rather fund a budget deficit using their credit line, even though they have cash in savings that they could use to pay it down. These individuals aren't irrational: they wish to use the outstanding debt as a constant reminder that they have to cut their spending. For example, they may have a $300 budget deficit, which has accumulated to a $3,000 credit line debt after 10 months. While they could pay down the $3,000 debt immediately using their personal savings, leaving the $3,000 in the credit line gives them a specific goal: Reduce the debt and resolve the deficit problem. By paying down the debt with savings, they feel they are ignoring the problem. But this is more psychological than anything else.

In other words, keeping the debt outstanding makes the deficit a short-term problem, rather than a long-term one.

But if at some point the individual concedes that his or her debt isn't going to decrease anytime soon, he or she would be better off to shift it into the source of borrowing that charges the lowest rate.

So here is a New Year's resolution: Continue spending, eating, and not exercising, as before. But go and sell some stocks and bonds, take out a line of credit secured against your home, or even collapse some of the RRSPs, and pay down the high-interest credit card debt.

Mutual Funds:
The Next Generation

31

For those of you who are unhappy with the tax implications of your mutual funds, and are willing to put some time and effort into finding an alternative, you might want to check out a new concept in managed investing. A new U.S. online product, called Folio, provides a glimpse of what the future of tax-efficient portfolio investing might look like. It's on its way to Canada as well.

Folios, which are sold by the company FOLIO*fn*, are a hybrid between a (very) discount brokerage account and a professionally managed mutual fund. It's a Web-based build-it-yourself mutual fund that allows you to either pick your own stocks or invest in a variety of pre-existing portfolios.

Each Folio can include up to 50 different stocks, picked from about 3,500 listed securities, which covers about 95% of the active market in the United States. The service also allows investors to access fresh investment advice and market reports, all in one place. Then, twice daily, at 10:15 am and 2:45 pm to be precise, the computer system matches the sell and buy orders from all the investors, and thus clears the order deck. Any outstanding orders are sent directly to the stock exchange. There is an added fee if you want to trade at other times during the day.

For example, if between 10:15 am and 2:45 pm a total of 500,000 orders to sell Microsoft accumulate, and 600,000 orders to buy accumulate as well, then the first 500,000 of the buy orders are satisfied using the 500,000 sell orders. The remaining 100,000 buy orders are sent directly to the stock exchange.

For investors without the time or experience to build and manage their own portfolios, there are several pre-existing Folios to choose from, such as a Dow30 Folio, a Biotech Folio, or an Ethical Folio. This is a far cry from using a discount brokerage, where you are taking a flyer on a couple of stocks. With Folios, the system encourages investors to diversify and think in terms of a larger portfolio. Hence, they can benefit from a strong diversification focus on the one hand, and enjoy flexibility and freedom of individual stock picks on the other.

Technically, the Folio system is a self-clearing broker–dealer subsidiary — the equivalent of what we did back in grade school when we traded hockey cards during recess. More important, this method of exchanging and redeeming your shares happens to be a lot more tax-efficient than owning a standard mutual fund, since you don't have a distant manager selling your appreciated stocks at will, which creates an unpleasant tax liability for you. With Folios, you can trade off winners against losers to neutralize most of your tax liability. You also avoid the hassle of selling each stock position at a time, since you can execute the batch trades.

The annual subscription cost for the service is about $450 Canadian, but that's not high when you compare the virtually unlimited number of trades you can perform, and the implicit costs you pay in a garden-variety mutual fund. Assume you have invested $25,000 in mutual funds. How much are you paying each year in management fees? As you can see from Table 18, with a portfolio worth $25,000, you are likely paying more than $450 annually in management fees, in the form of a Management Expense

TABLE 18
Funds and Their Fees in Canada:
Per $25,000 Investment

Annual Fees	# of Funds	% of Funds
< $125	412	9.0%
$125–$250	258	5.7%
$250–$375	281	6.2%
$375–$500	571	12.5%
$500–$625	962	21.1%
$625–$750	1333	29.2%
> $750	749	16.4%

Note: Does not include loads and sales charges.

Source: GlobeFund.com.

Ratio (MER). At the time I was conducting this research, there were 4,566 mutual funds available in Canada, and 29.2% of the funds had annual fees between $625 and $750. In total, 66.7% of Canadian mutual funds had annual fees equal to or greater than $500. So, the Folio subscription fee is comparatively inexpensive, especially to those with larger portfolios.

In sum, consumers who are too busy, bored and uninterested in managing their own investments will continue to rightfully outsource their finances to professionals and use mutual fund-like or wrap products managed by professional investment managers and their large management fees and tax bills.

The Rush To Leave:
Is There a Money Drain?

32

For a while it seemed like everybody wanted to get their RRSP money out of Canada. The recent convoy of money crossing the border went by the peculiar name of "clones" and was marketed quite aggressively by all the large mutual fund companies. As I mentioned in an earlier chapter, clones are 100% RRSP eligible funds that ostensibly invest in Canadian capital markets. But in reality, clone funds use derivative securities, such as futures contracts, to mirror the performance of investments offered outside Canada. In other words, the funds are "Canadian" in label only — the returns parallel the returns you'd receive on foreign markets. This isn't a secret: Fund managers proudly market their clone funds, and the foreign indexes they mirror. And there is nothing the government can do, without changing the RRSP rules.

Historically, you see, foreign content restrictions were legislated in order to protect and support Canadian capital markets. But as it stands now, we can completely bypass the tax restrictions using perfectly safe and legal derivative securities. With a bit of imagination, you can think of derivative securities as a novel layaway plan for stocks and bonds. I explained this concept in Chapter 7. Although your mutual fund is not holding any foreign content directly, an investment bank is holding it on the fund's behalf. Of course, the investment bank does not have any foreign content restrictions, and that's the trick.

But why is international investing so important? What's wrong with being patriotic with your nest egg? Is it simply because most other national stock markets have done better than Canada over the last 10 to 15 years? According to the Morgan Stanley Capital indices, Finland earned the highest return of all major stock markets in 1998, with a 139% effective annual return. So, should we all lobby Ottawa for a special RRSP Finland exemption? (Not to be confused with Norway, which lost 24.5% in 1998.)

But superior performance by some foreign markets alone can't explain the rush to get out of the Canadian stock market. After all, success in foreign markets requires accurate forecasts of which markets will perform well in any given time period. For every individual who chose to invest in Finland, someone else lost by investing in Norway. And even if Finland does well in one year, there is no guarantee that it won't perform terribly the next year.

Of course, hindsight is 20/20. It is always easy to look back and lament the fact that we were not allowed to place more of our tax-sheltered savings in the better markets. But it's impossible to predict, before the fact, which markets are "better" markets. Hence, we can't explain the rush to foreign markets using the "superior performance" argument exclusively. So what explains the desperation with which investors try to expose their tax-protected savings to foreign markets?

If I had a reliable crystal ball and knew that all world stock markets were expected to earn exactly 15% on average over the next year, I would still want to diversify internationally. You might wonder, why bother?

Investing internationally is important because of what we call "correlation", not "returns". The correlation effect refers to the reduction in risk caused by investing in more than a single asset class, and is the reason for the theoretical and empirical support for diversification.

Correlation describes the degree to which the returns associated with two different asset classes move together. Correlation values range from a high of one to a low of negative one. High *positive* correlation between two asset classes means that above-average returns by one asset class will be associated with above-average returns of the other, and vice versa. Conversely, high *negative* correlation means that above-average returns by one asset class will be associated with below-average returns by the other, and vice versa. Finally, zero correlation suggests that returns by one asset class are unrelated to the returns by the other.

The extreme cases, one and negative one, are referred to as "perfect correlations", and occur where returns are exactly the same (perfect positive correlation), or exactly the opposite (perfect negative correlation). These scenarios are unlikely, as different markets rarely, if ever, have identical or exact opposite performances. However, correlation scenarios between one and negative one are where reality lies.

Suppose you are faced with a choice between Canadian and U.S.-based investments, and both are expected to earn exactly 15% over the next year. Furthermore, assume that the United States and Canada are not perfectly correlated, which means the returns of both investments do not move exactly together in parallel. In other words, when U.S. investments perform well, the Canadian investments may or may not, and vice versa. With that said, I argue that you have much to gain by investing your money in both Canada and the United States — i.e., diversifying internationally — even though they both are expected to earn the same amount on average.

TABLE 19
Risk and Return: 50% Canadian, 50% American

Correlation between Markets	1-Year Probability of Shortfall
1.00	36.94%
0.75	35.33%
0.50	33.43%
0.25	31.11%
0.00	28.18%
–0.25	24.28%
–0.50	18.63%
–0.75	9.44%
–1.00	0.00%

Note: Both U.S. and Canadian Stock Markets are expected to grow at an annual rate of 15%, with a volatility of 30%.

Sounds paradoxical?

Table 19 explains my point. Assume that you invest 50% in Canada and 50% in the United States: What is the probability of earning *less than* a one-year 5% GIC? I will answer this question with the correlation scenarios listed in the table.

The table indicates that, with your investment divided equally between the Canadian and the U.S. markets, the probability of earning less than a 5% GIC depends on the strength of the movement between these two markets. In the extreme case where future correlation between Canada and the United States is a perfect 1.00 — the highest it can be, the probability of earning less than the GIC is roughly 37%. At the other extreme is the perfect opposite where correlation coefficient is a *negative* 1.00. In this case, the probability of earning less than a 5% GIC is reduced to zero. In other words, you will *never do worse* than the 5% GIC. You will always beat the risk-free rate. Now, in real life, of course, correlations between the United States and Canadian markets are much lower than 1.00 and much higher than negative 1.00. The key point is: By diversifying your investment in just two countries, you drastically reduce the risk of underperforming the 5% GIC.

As you can see, even though the correlation between the two investments is zero, the probability of earning less than a 5% GIC is reduced to about 28%, demonstrating the substantial benefits to diversify internationally.

Now you might ask, what is the actual correlation between U.S. and Canadian markets? How strong will the diversification effect be in the future?

As far as the United States and Canada go, the correlation number has ranged from 0.40 to 0.85, depending on the historical period in question.

What will it be, looking forward? It's tough to tell.

Unfortunately, the difficulty with correlations is that they seem to collapse when you need them most. In the early 1970s and 1980s, it was easy to locate international stock markets that moved independently or with relatively low correlation to Canada. Lately, it seems to be more difficult to locate low correlated markets. More precisely, during bull market cycles, different markets obey their historical correlations with each other. However, much to our regret, in bad times, when world markets are suffering, everybody and everything seems to go down at exactly the same time. In a climate of stress or investment shocks, correlation numbers tend to move towards plus one.

What's more, as international stock markets become increasingly integrated, capital flows more freely, and national protectionist regulations are further reduced, the odds become more likely that correlations will increase. No longer will the financial economies of Europe, North America and the Far East march to different drummers.

Indeed, diversification across economic sectors and industries will be more important than the nationality of those industries. Keep in mind, the goal is to locate good companies spread across the global economy. The flag they fly is secondary.

This, of course, does not mean that we should abandon or diminish the international side of our portfolio; rather, we simply have to be careful not to oversell the benefits of geography. A fully diversified portfolio will consider all characteristics that can be exploited for the correlation effect, and the resulting lower risk.

Remember, now that you can finally do it doesn't mean you should. As one acquaintance recently put it, Canada is virtually "on sale".

Do You Want to Be Your Pension Fund Manager?

33

I recently returned from a fascinating trip to Tallahassee, Florida. I had the distinct pleasure of participating in an unprecedented pension experiment. Over 600,000 public employees of the State of Florida were given the option of converting their Defined Benefit pension plan to a Defined Contribution pension plan. And, if they elected to switch, they would become managers of their personal pension fund; for better or for worse. Apparently, there is talk of the United States implementing a similar scheme for their sacred Social Security: If certain politicians have their way, individual taxpayers can self-direct their Social Security money, or choose to allow the government to manage it instead.

But, beneath this newfound financial liberty lurks the ugly face of downside risk. Beware of pension trustees offering conversion gifts!

So, here is a crash course on what you need to know about pensions. There are two basic categories of pension plan: defined contribution (DC) and defined benefit (DB). There are also some hybrids, but they are relatively minor players in the Canadian market.

The DB plan, as its name implies, is a pension where your retirement benefit is defined well in advance of your retirement date. For example, you might be promised 2% of your salary for each year of service. If you work for 30 years — at the same employer — your pension would be 60% of your last paycheque. The Canadian Pension Plan (CPP) is a good example of a DB plan. If the employer has promised you a pension benefit when you retire, they must set aside funds right now to pay for those promises in the future, and that's where the actuaries do their magic estimates of how much must be set aside.

The employer, or the financial institution through which the pension money is managed, takes all the risk in a defined benefit plan. Even if returns on investments are lower than expected over the next 30 years, the employer must still pony up the fixed percentage of the employee's salary, as promised in the DB plan. This is an advantage to the employee, who doesn't have to stay up nights wondering whether the pension is large enough to fund retirement — instead, the exact amount to be received is known to everyone.

But there are disadvantages to the employee as well, in terms of opportunity lost. For example, if markets experience tremendous growth between the contribution and retirement, the employee doesn't benefit at all — he or she continues to receive the fixed percentage of salary that makes up the defined benefit. As we will discuss further in this chapter, the employee is effectively "paying" for the elimination of risk with the elimination of opportunity beyond the benefits defined in the plan.

In contrast, DC plans are similar in concept to an RRSP. Your employer, perhaps matched by you, will deposit a percentage of your current salary in a tax-sheltered fund. Then, whatever that pot of money grows to by the time you retire will determine your pension annuity and retirement income. If the investments in the fund do well during the course of your working life, you gain. But, if the fund and its investments do poorly — and this is the key message — you will have a smaller pension. The risk is borne by you, the employee. However, DC plans also provide you opportunity unavailable in DB plans, in terms of potential growth. In addition, some DC plans allow you flexibility when choosing investments. Within the DC universe, you can have self-directed plans, where you control the asset allocation, investments and choices, or trustee-directed plans, where all the decisions are made for you. You will have the opportunity to fine-tune your portfolio to match your personal risk-tolerance level.

Now, let's return to the subject of pension conversions. At first glance, if a DB plan is holding $200,000 on behalf of your promised pension — also known by the actuaries as the accumulated benefits obligation — then giving you complete management control of the $200,000 in a DC self-directed account would appear like a fair deal. After all, you now make the decisions, and you control the asset mix.

However, you must remember that: While you will probably be investing in the same type of instruments the professional fund manager has at his or her disposal, you are also taking the risk that your portfolio will tank, leaving you living on cat food when you retire. Whereas, if the money were to remain in a DB-style plan, the plan sponsor or employer would be "on the hook" for the guaranteed pension annuity, if the fund manager happened to screw up.

So, should employees opt for DB plans if given the opportunity to do so? There is some evidence that employees should only do so if they are investment-savvy. In a study published in the *American Economic Review*, evidence is presented that many people saving towards their pension plan understand little about the consequences of their choices (see Benartzi and Thaler, 2001). The implication of this study is important: While we typically think that more choices is better, the reality of vast ignorance about how to manage one's portfolio suggests that giving people the

TABLE 20
The Pension Replacement Rate:
What fraction of your salary will you get when you retire?

@ Interest Rate*	Assuming This Fraction of Salary Is Contributed/Saved			
	5.0%	6.0%	7.0%	8.0%
4%	16%	19%	23%	26%
5%	22%	26%	30%	35%
6%	29%	34%	40%	46%
7%	38%	46%	53%	61%
8%	50%	60%	70%	81%
9%	66%	80%	93%	106%
10%	87%	105%	122%	140%

Assumptions:
Work for: 30 Years
Retire for: 30 Years

* During both accumulation and spending phases.

—————

Source: Author's non-stochastic calculations.

choice to manage their own pension fund may not be that good an idea.

But let's assume you are a sophisticated investor, and portfolio management comes second nature to you. Should you switch from the DC plan to the DB plan?

To evaluate the advantages and disadvantages associated with DC plans, it's important for employees to consider the downside risk. Table 20 provides a measure of this risk. For example, if you and/or your employer are contributing a combined total of 6% of your salary towards the provision of a retirement pension — and the fund earns a fixed 8% rate of return — you will get a pension that is 60% of your final/average wage. However, if your adroit money skills only earn you 7%, your replacement rate will drop to 46% of your salary. Now, that's the risk. The reward, of course, is the opposite direction. Do you like this gamble?

Indeed, the State of Florida partially compensated for the "lost" downside protection by giving participants the one-time option to return to the DB plan, if and when they so desire. In my opinion, similar protection should be given to all employees who are given the choice. Otherwise, it might not be worth it to "take the money and run".

To sum, should you ever face the choice, consider carefully before switching from a DB plan to a DC plan. The advantage of a DB plan is that there is very little risk; the disadvantage is that there is no opportunity for earnings beyond the defined amounts. While the opportunities and flexibility associated with DC plans may motivate employees to switch, it's important that employees recognize the gamble at the core of a DC plan — a gamble that will affect every month of the retirement.

Diversification:
Is Anybody Listening?

34

I wouldn't be surprised if the word *diversification* has appeared in more personal finance newspaper articles than the word *portfolio* or *investments*. I, too, am guilty of it in this book. Diversification, to a financial planner, is the equivalent of location to a real estate broker: They both capture the essence of their trade, and have become clichés in their own right. Financial planners, advisors, consultants and academics have been preaching the virtues of "not putting all your eggs in one basket", ever since. . . . well. . . . there have been eggs and baskets.

Technically, diversification is an investment strategy. The strategy is as follows: Do not invest your investment portfolio in a single asset. Instead, divide your portfolio funds across numerous assets and asset classes that are based on geography, industry, the lifecycle of the firm, and many other classifications.

By doing so, experts argue, you can decrease the risk of your portfolio *without decreasing your portfolio's expected return*. Since most people are risk averse — prefer less risks to more risks, holding everything else equal — diversification is an easy way to optimize their portfolios.

Given the rock-solid arguments in favour of diversification, we would expect the vast majority of investors to diversify their portfolios. Yet there is some indication that this is not the case in reality. A comprehensive study, by Yale University's W.

Goetzmann and Cornell University's A. Kumar, that tracked the behaviour of individual investors over a five-year period raises serious doubts as to whether anybody is actually listening to this seemingly tiresome advice.

The scholars obtained a database of more than 40,000 investment accounts, totalling close to $2.5 billion in assets, from a large discount brokerage in the United States, covering the time frame between 1991 and 1996.

Their intention was to measure the extent to which individual investors diversify their stock holdings and construct so-called efficient portfolios that balance risk and return across different industries and economic sectors. They were also interested in examining the personal characteristics of individuals who are more, or less, likely to diversify their portfolio holdings.

The results are revealing. First, while the average portfolio had almost US$36,000 invested, the median number of stocks in the portfolio was only three. Yes, three. In the most recent year of the data sample, more than 25% of investor portfolios contained only one stock, and more than 70% contained five or less "names". To make matters worse, these stocks tended to be clustered in the same industry and were, thus, not very diversified or well balanced. The most popular names were IBM, AT&T, Wal-Mart, Merck and Glaxo, which is consistent with the very large trading volume in these stocks.

The authors were able to track the evolution and performance of the brokerage accounts from the same period, and, as you can see from Table 21, investors have been getting better at diversifying over time. The level of concentration has been slightly reduced, and by 1996, more than 30% of the accounts have more than five stocks, while in 1991 the number was closer to 17%. But, this is a far cry from the 20 to 30

TABLE 21		
Number of Stocks in Portfolio	*Percent of Portfolios Year 1991*	*Percent of Portfolios Year 1996*
1	33.02%	25.50%
2	20.55%	17.37%
3	13.51%	12.01%
4	8.86%	9.30%
5	6.11%	6.59%
6–10	12.36%	17.40%
11–15	3.28%	6.13%
Over 15	2.31%	5.70%

Sample of over 40,000 discount brokerage accounts with over US$2.5 billion in aggregate.

Source: W. Goetzmann and A. Kumar, "Equity Portfolio Diversification," NBER Paper #8686.

names that most experts believe is needed for a properly constructed portfolio.

Interestingly, the data shows that older investors are more diversified than the younger ones, and so are the white-collar workers when compared to their blue-collar counterparts; while salary and income did not play a major (a.k.a. statistically significant) role in determining levels of diversification.

Now, how did the investors perform? Did the general lack of diversification result in superior or inferior performance?

To assess performance, comparison must be made to a benchmark portfolio that commonly uses an index such as the TSE 300 or S&P 500. The authors of the study then posed the following question: Where investors have the choice between picking stocks and passively investing in an index, how well did the average portfolio in the sample perform, relative to the benchmark index? Performance is measured using two variables: returns and volatility. The risk–return tradeoff argues that when comparing two portfolios, higher risk is acceptable if it is associated with higher returns, measured per unit of risk. However, if the high-risk portfolio has equal or lower returns than the low-risk portfolio, the performance of the high-risk portfolio is unsatisfactory.

Not surprisingly, the study found that the actual investment returns from the individual portfolios consistently lagged behind the major indices, and tended to be more volatile (i.e., risky) as well. This suggests that the individual portfolios performed quite poorly: investors would have received superior returns, with less risk, through investing passively in an index rather than the stocks they chose. Hence, not only did the portfolios lack diversity, the stocks selected also suggest the investors lacked the ability to make good stock picks.

The authors of the study further argue that while correlations between individual stocks are declining, individual securities, at the same time, are becoming more volatile in their daily movement. This is bad news, because it means that we have to work harder to find stocks that zig when others zag. The old rules of thumb dictating the size of a diversified portfolio must therefore be revised upwards as well. Hence, a portfolio that would be considered diversified in the past may require further diversification in the future.

Now, granted, some might argue that the data used in the above study — which is based on discount brokerage accounts in the United States — reflects "play money", and not an individual's beloved nest egg. Hence, maybe investors are more diversified than the study suggests, through other investment holdings.

This, however, does not appear to be the case. The researchers were careful to document that the average size of the portfolio in their sample was quite large compared to the annual income of the owner of the portfolio, so the account represented a non-trivial fraction of net worth. With the average account representing at least 100% of annual income, this was not casino money we are talking about.

Also, while the most recent numbers are unfortunately more than six years old — academic studies are notoriously slow to publish — the recent technology boom and bust only serves to confirm the authors' conclusion that individuals are practising inappropriate and naïve stock selection.

In sum, if the U.S. experience is of any indication to the Canadian situation — which I would agree with because we are sufficiently close to our southern neighbour when it comes to investor behaviour — while you may be tired of hearing about the importance of diversification, most people are *still* not listening. In fact, the recent Nortel and JDS meltdowns, and their relative size in the Canadian market, should make this lesson even more apparent north of the border.

Ethical Investing:
Can You Do Worse?

35

Is your RRSP misbehaving when you sleep? Is your money really green? These, and related questions, have taken centre stage with the recent emergence of ethical funds as an asset class.

To be quite honest, my thinking in the past has been that by limiting your portfolio to only the so-called ethical companies, you are doing yourself a financial disservice. It is akin to the arbitrariness of only investing in companies whose ticker symbol excludes the letters S or X. Sure, you might get lucky once or twice, but you have narrowed your financial choices, which is never a good strategy. Moreover, how does one even go about creating a proper screen that differentiates the righteous from the sinners? Is it not something in the eye of the beholder?

In practice, my personal bias has always been to get the best and highest (legal) return on my personal investment portfolio — with no artificial constraints on who and what can be purchased — and then use my investment gains to give charity, adopt a road or buy a forest.

Financial economists like to call this kind of thinking "separation theorems". Namely, that management should focus on finding investment projects that generate the highest net present value for the company. Shareholders can then decide what exactly to do with the dividends.

Others have taken the opposite view and argued that ethical-friendly companies are likely to outperform their sinful colleagues by virtue of their long-term and global outlook. For example, a company that provides in-house daycare to employees will boost morale and might increase productivity. Or, companies that avoid any involvement with tobacco and firearms might save on potentially crippling litigation costs.

Until recently, the debate was centred on theoretical arguments and scant empirical evidence. But, a newly released international study by researchers in the Netherlands is shedding new light on the question of whether ethical investors are penalized or rewarded by the capital markets.

The authors collected historical investment returns from more than 60 self-classified ethical funds from across 10 different countries. Unfortunately, their analysis did not include Canada, but I have tried to fill in some of the gaps. (See Table 22.)

The results are quite interesting. First, despite all the talk about ethical investing, the size of the ethical (retail) mutual fund market is not large. In the United States, which has the largest contingent of these types of mutual fund, only 2.26% of mutual fund assets are invested in ethical funds. In contrast, the size of the ethical market in France is smallest, with only 0.01% of assets, while Canada comes in a small but respectable 1.0%.

Nevertheless, and despite size, investors have over 500 ethical mutual funds to choose from on a global scale. Some have been around for over 20 years, while most others are johnny-come-latelies with only a few track-years to show.

The authors of the report discerned a few interesting points relating to ethical investment performance over time. As I alluded to earlier, there is a general perception that ethical funds do worse — on

TABLE 22
Ethical Funds around the World

Country	# of Ethical Funds	Invested Assets in Millions USD	% of All Funds
Belgium	26	602	0.80%
France	14	371	0.01%
Germany	22	1,317	0.04%
Italy	5	2,077	0.45%
Sweden	42	1,190	1.46%
Switzerland	22	1,011	1.12%
Netherlands	11	1,309	1.20%
United Kingdom	55	6,390	1.35%
Unites States	230	153,000	2.26%
Canada*	49	3,500	1.00%

Sources:
For international data, R. Bauer, K. Koedijk, and R. Otten, "International Evidence on Ethical Mutual Fund Performance and Investment Style" Working Paper. Available at SSRN.com.
* For Canadian data, Morningstar and Globe HySales.

average — than sinful funds. At the opposite end of the spectrum, ethical fund managers have claimed their performance is better, since they keep out the sinners.

But, it appears that neither of these claims is true on a consistent basis. These funds do not do worse, or better.

There are a few anomalies that are persistent, though. First, it seems that the investment performance of ethical funds in the U.K. is better than the performance of ethical funds in the United States, or the rest of Europe for that matter. Second, and more interesting, newer ethical funds tend to do worse than older funds. In other words, it seems to take some time before ethical funds can overcome the "loss" associated with restricting their investment opportunity set. Perhaps it is the lack of experience on the part of fund management, or "too strict" of an initial screening criterion, that limits the performance of start-ups. Thus, at first, the company may only be willing to do business (invest) with Mother Teresa — which obviously limits choices and performance — but over time, they lower their standards and improve their relative returns.

But, once you take all the evidence, as well as the pros and cons, into account, the authors' closing statement is telling. They said: "We find no evidence that investors are penalized for selecting ethical funds ... they are no better, or worse, than any other mutual fund."

In conclusion, the size of the ethical mutual funds market is still small, with limited choices and small track records. If they want to continue to attract investors' money — with more than just good deeds — they will have to work harder to show they can compete and distinguish themselves from the rest of the pack. And, more important, for the investors, wait for them to produce a reasonable track record before you open your wallet.

Do Posted Rates Mean Anything?

36

An old high school buddy of mine recently called to show off his new mortgage rate. It seems that he had managed to "negotiate" a full 1.25% off the posted five-year rate, and was quite proud of his financial acumen.

It appears that nobody is paying posted mortgage rates anymore. As any personal finance guru will endlessly carp, the first lesson in Mortgages 101 is to demand a reduction by threatening to take your business elsewhere.

So, is it time to sell short the bank stocks? Is their lucrative money gig up? Or, perhaps, are posted rates becoming as meaningless as the initial price at a Middle Eastern bazaar?

My suspicion — and one that is doubtless shared by many a bank visitor — is that financial institutions have recently been posting official mortgage rates that are slightly higher than what they originally intended, simply because so many consumers are refusing to pay those same posted rates. The banks realize they will be forced to settle for 50 to 150 basis points (or 0.5% to 1.5%) off the posted rates, and thus pad the numbers to begin with. Over time, this game has accelerated, since a growing number of shoppers are unwilling to accept the posted number as anything but an opening gambit. Hence an inflationary spiral in posted rates.

In other words, because banks know that Canadian consumers expect a rate cut when shopping for a mortgage, they structure their pricing with the rate cut in mind. Hence, you may feel you were lucky to receive the rate cut, or you may feel that your bargaining abilities are second to none. But before you try to use those bargaining abilities in another context, consider the possibility that everyone receives the rate cut.

With that said, can this theory be supported by data?

To check, I compared the average five-year mortgage rates *posted* by the banks to the average yield on risk-free government bonds of similar maturity.

I calculated the spread between the posted mortgage rates and the risk-free government bonds of similar maturity. This spread, which is always positive, can be taken as a rough proxy of what the bank is actually earning by lending you the money. They charge you the five-year mortgage rate — a.k.a. the retail rate — but they base rates on wholesale numbers in the bond market.

For example, the rate on risk-free government bonds may be 4%. To determine the mortgage rate, the bank adds a 2.5% spread. Hence, the resulting posted mortgage rate is 6.5%.

Technically, of course, the banks are actually lending you your own money, which you deposited in their coffers, and which is earning paltry interest in the savings, chequing and GIC accounts. But since an alternative to writing mortgages is risk-free investment in government securities, the rates associated with these securities act as a benchmark upon which to base riskier mortgage rates.

As you can see from Figure 13, the spread between posted mortgage rates and the appropriate yield in the bond market has been increasing over the last 50 months. Recently it has been as high as 3%,

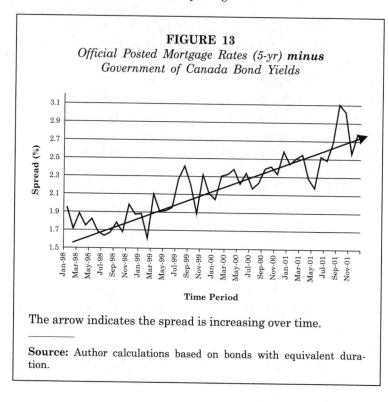

FIGURE 13
*Official Posted Mortgage Rates (5-yr) **minus**
Government of Canada Bond Yields*

The arrow indicates the spread is increasing over time.

Source: Author calculations based on bonds with equivalent duration.

whereas the same spread was closer to 1.5% a mere four years ago. In other words, the banks are asking you to pay relatively more than their benchmark for funds. But then, when you factor in the 0.5% to 1.5% reductions that many consumers demand, the banks are back where they started. Similarly, this is only for those customers that know to bargain. On the polite ones, banks actually make the bigger spread. So, net-net, the banks probably win.

Now, although there are a variety of competing explanations for this increasing spread over time, my "anticipatory padding" theory is backed up by various discussions with professionals in the mortgage business. Indeed, it seems that mortgage renewals pay higher spreads (i.e., get smaller discounts) than initiators, even though their threat to take business elsewhere isn't as credible.

Note, however, that if you decide to go with an open mortgage with a floating interest rate like the prime rate — of which, incidentally, I am a big fan — the banks don't have much room to embellish the posted numbers, and you are unlikely to get any concessions. You can think of it as getting transparency in exchange for rigidity.

Theories aside, the practical lesson from all of this should be quite clear. If you are currently negotiating a fixed mortgage with your bank, discard your ingrained Canadian politeness, fight hard and don't take anything less than a full point discount. But, you might want to reduce the size of the grin on your face.

Mutual Funds Rankings:
Should Taxes Matter?

37

I recently had the dubious pleasure of attending the intellectual equivalent of a celebrity wrestling match. The end result wasn't as bloody, though both sides certainly drew their lines in the sand. And, quite frankly, I'm having a hard time picking a winner.

I am talking, of course, about the debate surrounding income taxes and mutual fund returns, and whether fund companies should be forced to disclose pre-tax as well as post-tax numbers. Never heard of this fight? Well, soon, I'm sure, you will.

The issue goes something like this. When you buy a mutual fund, you are delegating the investment responsibility to a fund manager, who decides what stocks to buy and, more important, when to buy and sell them. If the manager buys and sells large quantities of stocks many times during the year — i.e., the fund has a high turnover rate — you will likely face a steep tax bill at the end of the year, *even if you didn't actually dispose of the fund units*. (Note: We are talking about mutual funds held outside of an RRSP.)

The root cause of this unpleasant tax liability is somewhat hidden from view, because the fund company tends to re-invest the distributions — which gave rise to your tax liability — back into additional units of the fund. So, it is not like you get a cheque from the fund company for the distributions, and are then required to pay some taxes. Rather, you actually get an annoying piece of T3 paper informing you that the fund company distributed funds to your account, but immediately used the funds to buy some additional units in the same fund. Hence, you don't see the funds distributed, but you are forced to pay tax on them.

For example, through buying and selling, a fund may generate $100. The $100 is not sent to you, but is used to purchase additional units in the same fund. The government demands you pay taxes on the $100 of distributions, even though you never receive a cent.

Paying income taxes on gains you have not actually realized yet may seem unfair — especially to those who are planning to hold on for the long run — but, the Income Tax Act makes it clear that all gains within mutual fund trusts and corporations must flow through to individual shareholders.

In fact, if you have the unfortunate luck to buy mutual funds before these so-called distribution dates, which are usually in the middle of December, you will have to pay tax on the $100 — which, to add insult to injury, is simply a return of your original principal!

Now, before you erupt in rage and storm out to dump tea in the nearest harbour, you might want to note that you are only pre-paying your taxes, and not paying any more than your fair share in total.

What do I mean? To explain, note that the amount of tax you pay when you finally sell the mutual funds is based on your adjusted cost base (ACB) — a calculation that determines the cost of an investment. The ACB is the total of the initial purchase price(s) of all the units plus any re-invested dividends, adjustments for redemptions and/or switches/transfers out, minus all transaction costs (e.g., commissions or fees). So, although you have to pay tax on distributions you did not receive, your tax liability at the time you sell the fund is also reduced because the

ACB would have been adjusted upwards to reflect the distributions.

Mutual funds that avoid turning over large quantities of stock in any given year tend to distribute less of these irritating realized gains, and therefore reduce your immediate tax bill. And while adjustments will take place when you sell the mutual funds, a rational investor will want to delay the tax bill as long as possible — particularly if liquid cash is tied up in investments. Further, the taxes associated with high turnover mutual funds are accelerated and thus can become substantial.

. Table 23 demonstrates how an investor would go about converting a pre-tax return to a post-tax

---

TABLE 23

Example of After-tax Return Calculation

Assume Investment of $10,000 on January 1st.
Assume Mutual Fund Earns 11.5% pre-tax during the calendar year.

Classification	Pre-Tax	Taxes Due	After-Tax Amount
Scenario one: capital gains realized			
Canadian Dividends	$300	@31% = $ 93	$207
Ordinary Interest Income	$150	@46% = $ 69	$ 81
Realized Capital Gains	$600	@23% = $138	$462
Total post-tax Investment Return:			$750
Scenario two: capital gains unrealized			
Canadian Dividends	$300	@31% = $93	$207
Ordinary Interest Income	$150	@46% = $69	$ 81
Realized Capital Gains	$600	@ 0% = $ 0	$600
Total post-tax Investment Return:			$888

return. Notice how critical the assumption is on unrealized gains.

Now back to the debate.

There are many in the fund industry who
strongly believe that consumers should be made aware
of tax-inefficient behaviour. If your manager is turning over the investments that make up the fund frequently — designated "churning" in the industry lingo
— you should be told, because your immediate tax
burden will be higher. Advocates of making this information public argue that through doing so, investors
can decide for themselves whether the tax implications are acceptable.

Interestingly, it seems that our U.S. cousins are
somewhat ahead of us on this matter. A large
number of research papers have demonstrated that
properly account for income taxes can completely
change the relative performance of a mutual fund.
Whereas one fund might perform much better than
another on a pre-tax basis, once taxes are paid, their
relative performance might completely reverse itself.
Fund A might be in the top quartile pre-tax, relative
to Fund B, but in the bottom quartile post-tax.

Of course, as an investor, we are only interested
in post-tax returns. After all, we can only consume
post-tax returns. Evaluating investment performance
on a pre-tax basis is as foolish as basing your personal budget on your gross earnings, not your after-
tax earnings. Pre-tax returns don't reflect your reality.

But do investors actually make their investment
decisions on a post-tax basis? In fact, some scholars have argued that many investors are completely
aware of the pre- versus post-tax difference. These
investors are directing their money to funds that do
better on an after-tax basis, as opposed to a pre-tax
basis. In other words, investors are standing up and
taking notice (see Bergstresser and Poterba, 2002).

These prompted the U.S. Securities and Exchange Committee (SEC) to force companies to disclose their tax efficiency in their annual reports, advertising and prospectus. Each fund must show how much it would have earned before taxes are paid, as well as after the government has received its share.

Needless to say, this new sunshine has disclosed some ugly warts. Some funds widely assumed to be high-performance do quite poorly on an after-tax basis.

So, with our southern cousins as guinea pigs, should all Canadian fund companies be forced to display this after-tax information on the premise that more information is better than less? Well, in a perfect world where everybody is rational and everything is costless, I would have to say: "Why not?" After all, how could it possibly hurt to have more information, rather than less?

While I do believe that investors are rational, providing additional information is not costless. Unfortunately, any additional administrative burden associated with determining both pre- and post-tax returns will be borne by the investing public in the form of higher management fees and expenses. And our expenses are high enough already.

Furthermore, even if the companies were to disclose after-tax numbers, they would have to base those numbers on a representative investor. In other words, since the fund managers can't provide custom fund reports for each customer — the costs would be prohibitive — they have to make certain assumptions regarding the nature of the fund unit holder. But who is the representative investor? Should it be the wealthy Ms. Smith in Alberta, or the poor Mr. Jones in Quebec? Their tax rates are quite different, and so will their after-tax returns be.

The debate continues.

So, the best we can do is make sure those fund companies that choose to compute, report and then advertise after-tax returns do so in an honest and unbiased fashion. Fund companies that choose not to should make it easier for investors who desire to do so themselves. How the industry will provide this information, and integrate investors into the process, is uncertain. However, as investment managers compete for investment funds to manage, solutions will be found that best balance the conflicting objectives and needs.

In sum — as one of my colleagues continuously reminds me — the historical returns you see advertised on TV and in your newspapers may not accurately reflect the number of chocolate bars you will be able to eat from the gains. If the money is sitting within an RRSP, half the money could go to Ottawa. And, if the funds are sitting outside of a tax shelter, then you certainly might want to pay attention to tax efficiency.

Taxes matter!

Investing in Education

38

Another year comes and goes and the academic term is starting yet again for us business school professors, and the new generation of MBA students are still lining up in droves to earn their advanced degrees. Many of them have temporarily given up lucrative jobs and successful careers to spend the next 16–24 months attending classes and doing homework. They have exchanged one set of difficult bosses and demanding assignments for another set of deadlines and stresses. And, to add insult to injury, they are sure to have to pay a pretty penny for this "job". In fact, I'm sure that each and every one of them will, at some point during their sojourn, wonder: "Why did I do this?"

I, too, often wonder whether an MBA — or, for that matter, any graduate degree — provides a decent return on equity. After all, going back to school is an investment in human capital. The cost of the investment is the tuition and expenses, plus any foregone wages, while the dividends and returns will (it's hoped) come from future salary increases and bonuses.

So, is going back to school a good move for you? Is it worthwhile to leave a decent paying job and relatively stable income to return to the hallowed halls of academia?

Well, it is quite difficult to generalize across different degrees, occupations and personal circumstances. After all, while an advanced degree in engineering, law, business or medicine is quite likely to result in better employment opportunities, the same cannot be said of graduate degrees in anthropology or Latin.

But here is one way to calculate for yourself.

Start with your current salary of $50,000, for example. If you go back to school for two years — which is a reasonable average, when the summers are taken into account — your approximate foregone wages will be $100,000. Thus, your colleague in the cubicle next door, who stays put, will be $100,000 ahead of you, if and when you come back to work. Then, add the actual cost of the education — for example, $60,000 for a medium priced MBA and textbooks — and you arrive at a total investment (ignoring some timing and tax issues) of $160,000.

Of course, some people will have to borrow a substantial portion of that money — perhaps using government guaranteed student loans, or from friends and relatives — and others will be lucky enough to tap into savings. But the underlying economics are the same, whether you are borrowing the money or using your own. You are investing hard earned money in an education — and make sure you remind your professor of that when he or she is putting you to sleep with abstract theories — and you expect to earn something above and beyond what you invested.

Of course, gratification is not instant, and it is highly unlikely that your salary will jump by $160,000 — from $50,000 to $210,000 — in your first year back at work to cover all the costs in the above example. It will, obviously, take some time to recoup the expenses. However, if you amortize (or spread) this "cost" over the remainder of your working life, the initial increase in salary needed to justify the investment is, surprisingly, not that large. In Table 24 you will see that a modest 11.7% increase in sal-

TABLE 24

By How Much Does Your 'Salary Have to Increase to Justify Going Back to School?

Current Salary	Total Cost in $ of Obtaining the Advanced Education				
	20,000	*40,000*	*60,000*	*80,000*	*100,000*
25,000	10.2%	13.1%	16.1%	19.0%	21.9%
50,000	8.8%	10.2%	11.7%	13.1%	14.6%
75,000	8.3%	9.2%	10.2%	11.2%	12.2%
100,000	8.0%	8.8%	9.5%	10.2%	10.9%

Note: Based on two years of graduate education, a 3% real wage growth, and all salary gains amortized over a 20-year career.

ary — pre- versus post-education salary — would be enough to pay for the investment over your remaining working life.

The intuition for this result is as follows. Sure, you have invested a total of $160,000 in your education, but remember the monetary cost and the time cost of foregone wages. If you take a long-term view and are willing to spread the gain over time, the initial gain does not have to be as high.

Of course, Table 24 can be used for any other range of values as well. For example, if you are currently earning $25,000 per year and want to pursue a graduate degree that will cost $100,000 to complete, then — as intuition would dictate — your graduating salary must be at least 21.9% higher, with an above-and-beyond-the-normal growth rate over the period. If you don't think you will be able to re-enter the labour force and earn at least 21.9% more than what you would have been making had you stayed, it might not be worth the investment.

Notice that, as you might expect, the greater the cost of the education, the greater the threshold, in terms of the size of the new salary, to make it worthwhile to invest in education. Also, the greater your current salary — all else being equal — the lower the threshold for the new salary, since even a small increase on your (large) salary will pay for the education.

And, for all the techies and spreadsheet gurus reading this, here is how the calculation was conducted. I first estimated the graduating salary, which would grow every year at the real-wage growth rate. I then calculated its present value that would exactly compensate for the lost wages and the cost of education. So, if the estimated present value of your new salary when you graduate is $1,000,000, and the present value of your old salary — had you not gone back to school — is only $800,000, then you can afford to pay up to $200,000 for your education.

Now, like any mathematical model, I have made certain implicit assumptions, such as a 20-year career after graduation and a 3% real-wage growth. But the intuition would be the same regardless of the exact parameters. The longer you expect to work, the greater the growth rate in the new salary path, and the lower the new salary has to be to justify the investment.

Of course, for those who are pursuing an education for the sake of an education — such as many of the liberal arts and more abstract disciplines — the value and return on investment can actually be infinite in satisfaction. In fact, many academic purists would rightly object to such a harsh economic analysis, by arguing that the psychic and societal value of education and knowledge can and should not be quantified. But my experience is that many prospective students *do* think in terms of risks and rewards, and such an analysis will have some value.

The financial lesson from this should be quite clear, although I must admit it is self serving. Investing in education pays off over time, though not immediately upon graduation. In fact, a recent study by P.T. Pereira and P.S. Martins (2002) makes the same point. Investing in education is risky, but for the most part has a positive expected return. Therefore, as long as you anticipate a moderate raise in salary from your new degree, it is probably worthwhile going back to school when you think of the long term.

The Time and Value of
Life Insurance

39

I recently saw a clever advertisement by a life insurance company in which a father is seen doting on his cute young son, with the tagline "your need for life insurance is growing".

I do agree that a family growing in size creates a demand for more life insurance. But as your children and loved ones age, your demand for life insurance should decline, not increase.

For those of you who are puzzled, here is a quick review on how much life insurance you need, and why, as your kids age, you need less.

First, here are some basics. Life insurance is not a consolation prize for the survivors. It is a risk management instrument just like your home, car and medical insurance. You must ensure you have enough, but you shouldn't buy more than you need, since the premiums could be better spent and/or invested elsewhere. (There are some tax advantages, which I have mentioned in earlier chapters.) Second, and more important, life insurance requirements are not a science, but an art. There is no mathematical formula to determine how much you need.

Some commentators advocate an insurance approach that is based solely on your salary or annual income — for example, coverage should be five or perhaps 10 times your salary; but I think that's the wrong way to go about it. Think about it: You may be particularly blessed with a salary that is much higher than what you require to live on. So why insure that entire amount? On the contrary, and more important, your salary might *not* be enough to support your family in the long run and, therefore, focusing on salary might also provide a distorted (and downward biased) picture of your needs.

In fact, a comprehensive study conducted by Professor Laurence Kotlikoff and some colleagues at Boston University (forthcoming in the *American Economic Review*) discovered that although Americans on average have sufficient life insurance, there is a "startling mismatch between insurance holdings and underlying vulnerabilities. For many of those with the greatest vulnerabilities, the amounts purchased are surprisingly small, and for many of those with the smallest vulnerabilities, the amounts purchased are surprisingly large". It seems that the relatively old and rich are buying too much, while the relatively young and poor are not buying enough.

So, I would argue that people are not thinking properly when it comes to life insurance needs and responsibilities.

I believe it is more appropriate to model insurance needs in terms of your dependants' financial vulnerabilities (DFV).

From a purely economic point of view, you are a (human) capital asset that produces large annual dividends. Those dividends comprise wages and salary, which then go towards funding your personal lifestyle as well as the liabilities generated by your dependent family and loved ones. Thus, maintaining your personal lifestyle would not be a concern when your life ends; however, the liabilities generated by your dependants would continue to require funding.

You must therefore purchase life insurance to cover this "gap" in funding. If something happens to you, the life insurance payment will step in to continue covering the expenses.

TABLE 25

Prudent Amount of Life Insurance =
The Present Value of Your Dependants' Financial Vulnerability

Real Yearly Exposure	Number of Years of Exposure				
	5	10	15	20	25
$10,000	$ 44,833	$ 82,128	$113,153	$ 138,962	$ 160,432
$50,000	$224,163	$410,639	$565,765	$ 694,810	$ 802,160
$75,000	$336,245	$615,959	$848,647	$1,042,215	$1,203,240

Assumption: 3.75% after-inflation after-tax discount rate.

Source: Author calculations.

The present value of your dependants' financial vulnerability — i.e., the amount of life insurance you should prudently have — depends on two dimensions. The first is the magnitude of the exposure, and the second is the time horizon of the exposure.

Say, for example, you have three young girls all under the age of six, whom you would like to support for the next 20 years. You estimate that their total annual maintenance costs are an average real (after-inflation) $75,000. In that case, Table 25 says that, today, you require $1,000,000 in life insurance. Of course, in five years from now, the liability horizon will decline to 15 years, and you will only require $850,000 of life insurance. In 10 years, the liability will decrease to $615,000.

Therefore, make sure to buy life insurance in relatively short-term bundles, so you can scale down (or up) as needed over time. In other words, don't commit to paying premiums on $1,000,000 in life insurance for the next 25 years, since in all likelihood your need for insurance will decline. Personally, I would recommend five-year increments and re-evaluate whenever the policy is up for renewal.

The finance theory underlying the above calculation is that: In the event of your demise, the (tax free) life insurance payout should be enough to purchase a period-certain annuity that will fund all future liabilities. Once your dependants' financial vulnerability disappears — think of an empty nest — there is no need for life insurance, at least for risk management purposes.

Of course, income taxes add another wrinkle to the discussion, since there are ways to build up wealth in a tax sheltered manner inside a life insurance policy that are difficult to replicate using conventional savings instruments. But these added quirks should definitely not be the main reason to buy life insurance — especially when you are starting to build a family. Your first priority should be to cover the liabilities in a prudent and economical manner.

In sum, Bill Gates does not require life insurance, even though his annual income probably exceeds the GNP of a small country. The key is liabilities, net of assets. So, take some time to measure the financial vulnerability of your dependants. Then, make sure you have enough life insurance; or, for that matter, make sure that you don't have too much. Incidentally, the same general approach applies to disability or critical illness insurance.

Jewish High Holidays:
A Time to Invest?

40

Although the size of my fellow Jewish tribe in North America is less than 2% of the general population, it is quite clear that their influence goes far beyond their small numbers.

As with their edgy humour, ethnic food and liberal politics, the Jewish holidays — with colourful names like Rosh Hashana, Yom Kippur, Chanukah and Passover — have become part of mainstream North American culture.

In my neighbourhood, many schools, stores and restaurants close their doors during these festive days, especially if they are affiliated with the Jewish community.

At the risk of alarming conspiracy theorists, the Jewish community also participates in a significant manner in the stock market.

Interestingly, although the national and international stock exchanges remain open for business during Jewish holidays, the volume of shares traded on the markets tends to be much lower than normal. It seems that a disproportionate number of money managers and stock traders are away from work those days, busy listening to — or dozing through — the Rabbi's sermons at their local synagogues.

Indeed, this "low volume" factoid is most marked on the New York Stock Exchange (NYSE) around the Jewish high holidays — which are based on the lunar calendar, but generally fall in September. Trading volume can be 25% less than normal.

But what is less known, and much more intriguing, is the actual behaviour of the stock markets during the holidays. After all, despite the reduced volume, they *do* remain open for business. But new evidence suggests that, on average, stock markets do not behave the same way on certain Jewish holidays as they would on a regular day.

Recently, two well-known financial scholars at the University of California sifted through data and discovered the exact nature of the influence Jewish holidays have on investment returns on the larger stock markets.

To understand the results of the study, however, you would require a working knowledge of finance as well as some basic knowledge of Judaism. Here is a crash course on all you ever wanted to know about the Jewish holidays. For those who found their Bar Mitzvah lessons too painful, I'll keep this brief.

Rosh Hashana is the Jewish New Year. It's less of a time of celebration than the New Year that falls on January 1. Instead, it's a two-day holiday associated with reflection and optimism towards the future. The evidence presented in the study suggests that markets have adopted this optimism as well, and tend to move higher during this holiday.

In contrast, Yom Kippur is a formal Day of Atonement. It is a sombre, reflective and weakening day, when members of the Jewish community will fast and spend the day praying until sundown. Amazingly, the study shows the stock markets actually drift lower during the Yom Kippur period. The market is in a bearish frame of mind. Hence, for many Jewish individuals checking their poor portfolio returns on the day following Yom Kippur, the first thoughts may be that their atonement was not accepted!

While I am certain to receive many emails in reaction to this chapter — perhaps even questioning my psychological classification of these holidays — the fact is that Rosh Hashana is associated with a brighter frame of mind than is Yom Kippur.

Why the Dow Jones Industrial Average should care is another question. But the evidence is significant: markets perform better than average on Rosh Hashana, and worse than average on Yom Kippur.

For comparison purposes, the authors analyzed another Jewish holiday, called Chanukah, which is meant to celebrate ancient Jewish history, and is associated with fewer restrictions or synagogue-based rituals.

And, as one would expect markets to rise based on the above-mentioned theory, but unlike the high holidays, they found a negligible influence on markets. This is, however, consistent with the fact that Chanukah tends to be celebrated at night — over scrumptious fried dumplings — *after* the markets have closed.

Table 26 presents a list of the trading volume and returns on Rosh Hashana, Yom Kippur, and Chanukah. The values reported in the Trading Volume column refer to the percentage difference in shares traded on the holiday associated with each row and the average daily volume. The values reported in the Returns column refer to the percentage difference between the annualized returns for the holiday and the annual return. "Annualized" refers to the process through which daily returns are adjusted to make them comparable to annual returns.

For example, on Rosh Hashana, trading volume is 17% less than the typical daily trading volume. However, the return on Rosh Hashana is 5% greater than normal returns, on an annualized basis. Compare these results to Chanukah, where the differences

TABLE 26
The Impact of Jewish High Holidays

Volume and Returns Relative to Rest of Year

Holiday	Trading Volume (Relative to typical daily trading volume)	Returns (Annualized holiday returns, relative to annual return)
Rosh Hashana = Jewish New Year	−17.0%	+5%
Yom Kippur = Day of Atonement	−13.0%	−3%
Chanukah = Celebrating History	−0.5%	+0%

Source: L. Frieder and A. Subrahmanyam, "Non-Secular Regularities in Stock Returns: The Impact of the High Holy Days on the U.S. Equity Market," Anderson School Working Paper, University of California.

are negligible: trading volume is only 0.5% less than normal, and returns are no different.

Okay. Now, some of you holiday buffs might be wondering: "Hey! What about Passover?" In fact, the authors looked at this too, but because Easter and Good Friday — both of which are based on the lunar calendar as well — tended to fall around the same time of year, they had a tough time disentangling the Jewish from the Christian effect.

In sum, whether or not you are headed to synagogue that day, you might want to "go long" around the Jewish New Year (Rosh Hashana), then "go short" around the Day of Atonement (Yom Kippur), and simply buy and hold over Chanukah.

Bibliography

Barber, B.M., and T. Odean. 2001. "Boys will be Boys: Gender, Overconfidence, and Common Stock Investment," *Quarterly Journal of Economics* 116, 1 (February): 261–92.

Barclay, M.J., and T. Hendershott. 2001. "Price Discovery and Trading after Hours," University of Rochester. Available online: <www.afterhourstrading.com>.

Benartzi, S., and R. Thaler. 2001. "Naïve Diversification Strategies in Retirement Plans," *American Economic Review*.

Bergstresser, D., and J. Poterba. 2002. "Do after-tax returns affect mutual fund inflows?" *Journal of Financial Economics*, 63.

Cadsby, T. 2000. *The Power of Index Funds*. Toronto: Stoddart Publishing.

Chalmers, J.M., R.M. Edelen, and G.B. Kadlec. 2000. "The Wildcard Option in Transacting Mutual-Fund Shares," Working Paper #00-03. Wharton School of Business, Financial Institutions Center.

Charupat, N., J. Dhaene and M.A. Milevsky. 2002. "When is it Optimal to Hedge against Death and Taxes?" Working Paper, Schulich School of Business.

Charupat, Narat, and Moshe Milevsky. 2001. "Mortality Swaps and Tax Arbitrage in the Annuity Market," *Journal of Risk and Insurance* 68, 2 (June): 124–47.

Coval, J., and T. Shumway. 2001. "Expected Option Returns," *Journal of Finance* (June).

Domian, D.L., and M.F. Racine. 2002. "Wealth and Risk from Leveraged Stock Portfolios," *Financial Services Review*, 11 (Spring).

Edwards, F.R., and M.O. Caglayan. 2001. "Hedge fund and commodity fund investments in bull and bear markets," *Journal of Portfolio Management* (Summer).

Elton, E., and M. Gruber. 1995. *Modern Portfolio Theory*. New York: John Wiley.

Frieder, L., and A. Subrahmanyam. 2002. "Non-Secular Regularities in Stock Returns: The Impact of the High Holy Days on the U.S. Equity Market," Anderson School Working Paper, University of California.

Goetzmann, W., and A. Kumar. 2001. "Equity Portfolio Diversification," NBER Paper #8686. NBER.

Gross, D., and N. Souleles. 2002. "An Empirical Analysis of Personal Bankruptcy and Delinquency," *Review of Financial Studies* (Spring).

Kotlikoff, L. with B. Douglas Bernheim, Lorenzo Forni, and Jagadeesh Gokhale. Forthcoming. "The Mismatch Between Life Insurance Holdings and Financial Vulnerabilities: Evidence from the Health and Retirement Survey," *American Economic Review*.

Markowitz, Harry. 1991. "Individual versus Institutional Investing," *Financial Services Review* 1.

Milevsky, M.A. 2001a. "Mortgage Financing: Floating Your Way to Prosperity," The IFID Centre Research Paper #01-01. Available online at <www.the-ifid-centre.ca>.

———. 2001b. "Optimal Annuitization Policies: Analysis of the Options," *North American Actuarial Journal* 5, 1 (January): 57–69.

Milevsky, M.A., and A.A. Gottesman. 2002. *Insurance Logic*. Toronto: Stoddart Publishing.

Milevsky, M.A., and S. Posner. forthcoming 2003. "A Continuous-Time Analysis of the Risks and Rewards from Dollar-Cost Averaging," *International Journal of Theoretical and Applied Finance*.

———. 2001. "The Titanic Option: Valuation of Guaranteed Minimum Death Benefits in Variable Annuities and Mutual Funds," *Journal of Risk and Insurance* 68, 1 (March): 55–79.

Milevsky, M.A., with C. Robinson. 2000. "Self-Annuitization and Ruin in Retirement," *North American Actuarial Journal* 4, 4 (October): 112–29.

Pesando, J.E., and P.M. Shum. 1999. "The Returns to Picasso's Prints," *Journal of Cultural Economics*, vol 23.

Poterba, J., J. Shoven, and C. Sialm. 2000. "Asset Location for Retirement Savers," Working paper #7991, Stanford University and the National Bureau of Economic Research.

Runkle, D.E. 1988. "Why no crunch from the crash," Federal Reserve Bank of Minneapolis *Quarterly Review* (Winter): 2–7.

About the Author

Moshe Arye Milevsky is a tenured finance professor at the Schulich School of Business at York University in Toronto, Canada. He is also Executive Director of the Individual Finance and Insurance Decisions (IFID) Centre at the Fields Institute. The focus of his teaching, research and consulting work is in the interplay of investment management, personal finance and insurance. In addition, Moshe Arye is also author of the best selling *Money Logic: Financial Strategies for the Smart Investor* (Toronto: Stoddart, 1999); co-author of two other books, *Insurance Logic: Risk Management Strategies for Canadians* (Toronto: Stoddart, 2002) and *The Probability of Fortune* (Toronto: Stoddart, 2000); editor of the *Journal of Pension Economics & Finance* (Cambridge: Cambridge University Press) and contributing editor of the *National Post Business* magazine, in which he writes a popular column on finance.

Moshe Arye lives in Toronto with his wife Edna and three daughters, Dahlia, Natalie and Maya. You can download copies of Moshe's recent research articles at <www.yorku.ca/milevsky> or you can email him at <milevsky@yorku.ca>.